S0-CCI-922

Edited by Marcella Vasconi

THE BOOK OF

The Great History of VENICE

THE 1,200-YEAR-OLD HISTORY OF THE VENETIAN REPUBLIC

DEMETRA

Design, layout and editing: Sedigraf, Blevio (CO)
Illustrations: Diego Pasquino
Photographs: Sedigraf archives. Many thanks to Davide Sala for their help in the iconographic research. Sedigraf is willing and ready to pay the amount due for the pictures of unknown source published in this book.

The book of THE GREAT HISTORY OF VENICE
1ª edizione dicembre 1997

Via Strà, 167 – S.S. 11
37030 Colognola ai Colli (VR)
Tel. 045/6174111 - Fax 045/6174100

Introduction

Unique and graced with a charm all its own, Venice, famous the world over, is today a popular destination with tourists and travelers alike. The former, although often on fast-paced schedules, are nevertheless entranced by the "magic" of the city's canals, bridges, *calli*, churches and buildings, and depart taking with them dreamlike images. The latter, usually more attentive, even take in the city's most out-of-the-way recesses and less eye-catching – but no less charming – sights, trying their best to capture its myriad secrets. To both – the distracted tourist and the observant traveler – this book is addressed, the aim of which is to trace Venice's rich thousand-year history in order to highlight the reasons underlying the city's unique character.

Initially a refuge for mainland inhabitants threatened by "barbarian" invaders, from the very outset Venice was able to fully exploit its location on the lagoon, transforming such a hostile environment into a thriving center, rich in craft and trade activities, and capable of governing itself autonomously, at a time when the rest of Europe was still under the yoke of feudalism. Bridging East and West, the Venetian Republic played an important role as an intermediary, and developed to the extent of becoming an extremely popular venue with princes and emperors, and of expanding its dominions over the entire Mediterranean, as far as the very heart of the Eastern Empire.

Venice's seafaring and mercantile calling, her love for the arts and culture, and her readiness to accept what other people had to offer, for centuries helped shape a lively environment, a melting-pot of races and ethnic groups, a place where not only goods, but also ideas were constantly being exchanged. If after Napoleon's "betrayal" the Serenissima lost her independence, letting her history become a part of Italy's, traces of her glorious past still remain to bear witness to her former grandeur. The first part of this volume offers the reader a chronological history of the city, starting from its origins – even the legendary – and goes up to the end of the 19th century. The second part, divided by a basic chronology, consist of monographic essays on some of the salient features of Venice's rich culture, starting from what can be viewed and admired by one and all: such well-known places, for example, as Saint Mark's Square and environs, or the Grand Canal, or even the lagoon's lesser islands; both the major arts – with their illustrious representatives from Canaletto to Goldoni – and the minor, the craftsmanship of which – like Murano glassware – is alive and vibrant in every corner of the city, and indeed throughout the world; and lastly, events, such as the Carnival, or the pageantries which to this very day the city has never ceased to celebrate.

A Unique Lagoon

VENICE springs from one of the numerous lagoons on the northeastern coast of Italy. It is the result of layer upon layer of sediment which has been brought to the area over the centuries from the Po, to the south, the Timavo to the north and from other rivers that together have contributed to the formation of the PO VALLEY and to the region of VENETO. The area is surrounded by the Adriatic Sea and outlined by its "*tomboli*" – the narrow shorelines which the ancient Roman historian **Titus Livius** described. The lagoons were rich with salt water and small islands which were subject, not only to the movements of the sea, but also to earth tremors which, in some cases, were particularly violent.

The motion of the rivers and the sea and **the movements of the earth** have all contributed, though in different measures, to the formation of a **unique terrain**. This terrain is characterized by narrow strips of solid earth and sand which were carried in by streams of fresh water that isolated the saltwater. At some points these areas were particularly deep, in others, less so, and from them, firm ground and marshes were formed.

An interesting view of the Venetian lagoon of today.

If we were to take a trip into the past, before man began making changes, we would be able to observe many differences, for example, the **large areas of reeds** which were reflected in the calm, clear waters; the quiet "*barene*" – **marshy areas** covered with sparse vegetation; the "*motte*" – **higher sandy ground**; the "*velme*" – **vast muddy tracts** and finally the **shallows** which were determined by the whims of the sea.

Man's intervention over the course of the centuries **has sensibly modified the territory** by improving vast areas of its coastline and by adding to its natural land mass.

Some of the smaller islands were transformed into larger bodies of land which were connected by bridges and developed into the city we now know as Venice – the Mecca of international tourism. Other islands like MURANO, BURANO and TORCELLO, which lie farther from the historical center, have maintained a rich and vital presence; other tiny islands are hidden from most of us, like precious jewels; some others are uninhabited today although they boast a glorious past; still others have sunk back into the sea leaving us only documentation to remember them by. The shorelines were finally reinforced to prevent the sea from creating further damage to the internal islands.

To better understand the complex **structure of the territory** in which this glorious Republic was developed, it is a good idea to look at the vast area of lagoons from above. In this way we can observe how the lagoons form a virtual labyrinth, inside of which, few are able to navigate with confidence.

The coastline is bordered on the east by JESOLO and to the south by CHIOGGIA from which begins the fifty kilometers of coastline which separates the lagoon from the sea. Inside this basin, almost at the **center**, the one hundred and more islands of **historical Venice** emerge and are divided by a network of more than one hundred and fifty canals. The islands are united by more than four hundred bridges and connected

Veneto's lagoon, in an image from the last century.

A panoramic plan of Venice from the 16th century.
On the next page: *a plan of Veneto's lagoon today.*

to the mainland at MESTRE by the **Ponte della Libertà** (Liberty Bridge). To the southeast of this nucleus, lie the islands of **Giudecca** and the tiny **San Giorgio** which are reachable within a few minutes by crossing the wide canal. This **built up area**, shaped in the form of a fish (a little more than seven square kilometers large), is marked by the presence of the **Grand Canal**, which was probably at one time an ancient riverbed. The canal **almost symmetrically divides the two parts of the lagoon**.

Toward the south, the wider coastline is protected from the sea by the shores of LIDO and PELLESTRINA which are separated by the **Port of Malmocco**. To the north, the lagoon is defended from the sea by the LITORALE DEL CAVALLINO which goes as far as the **Port of Piave Vecchia** near the shoreline of Jesolo.

Inside the southern lagoon, between the historical nucleus of Venice and the shoreline of Lido, **appear a number of**

small islands. A good part of these are arranged along three horizontal lines: the GRAZIA and SAN SERVOLO; SACCA SÈSSOLA, SAN CLEMENTE and SAN LAZZARO DEGLI ARMENI; SANTO SPIRITO and LAZZARETTO VECCHIO. Further south, in the direction of the Port of Malmocco and Chioggia, in proximity to the shorelines, lie the islands of POVEGLIA, OTTAGONO ABBANDONATO and OTTAGONO ALBERONI. Closer to the shoreline, beginning at the Ponte della Libertà, TREZZE, SAN GIORGIO IN ALGA, SANT'ANGELO DELLA POLVERE, the EX BATTERIA PODO, the EX BATTERIA POVEGLIA and the EX BATTERIA FISOLO emerge from the waters.

Inside the northern lagoon, between the historical nucleus of Venice and the Litorale del Cavallino and bordered on the left by a series of swamps, a number of small islands arise. Most of these islands are full of life and among the most famous.

From the Ponte della Libertà, in the part of the lagoon which is nearest to the mainland, the small islands of SAN SECONDO, CAMPALTO, TESSERA, CARBONARA and LOVO are aligned from east to west. In the same direction, just to the south, are the islands of SAN MICHELE, MURANO, the tiny SAN GIACOMO IN PALUDE, and MADONNA DEL MONTE. Still farther south, FORTE SANT'ANDREA, SANT'ERASMO, along with LAZZARETTO NUOVO and SAN FRANCESCO DEL DESERTO, all constitute a real and proper internal coastline. Beyond this, we find BURANO, adjacent to MAZZORBO, and, the most isolated, TORCELLO, immersed between the **Palude della Rosa** (Marshes of the Rose) and the marshes of **Centrega,** divided by the islands of SANT'ARIANO, SANT'ANDREA and SANTA CRISTINA.

The climate in Venice is obviously **very humid** and sometimes subject to **fog**, but the winter weather is modified by the activity of the ADRIATIC SEA which, from August to March, maintains a warmer temperature than the air. The **winds** which most affect the climate are the **north-east wind**, the **Bora** (much less violent than in TRIESTE) and the **Sirocco** – guilty of bringing humidity and rain and therefore contributing to the **phenomena of the high water levels** – a serious problem which torments the city and inspires many technicians, scientists and politicians to get involved.

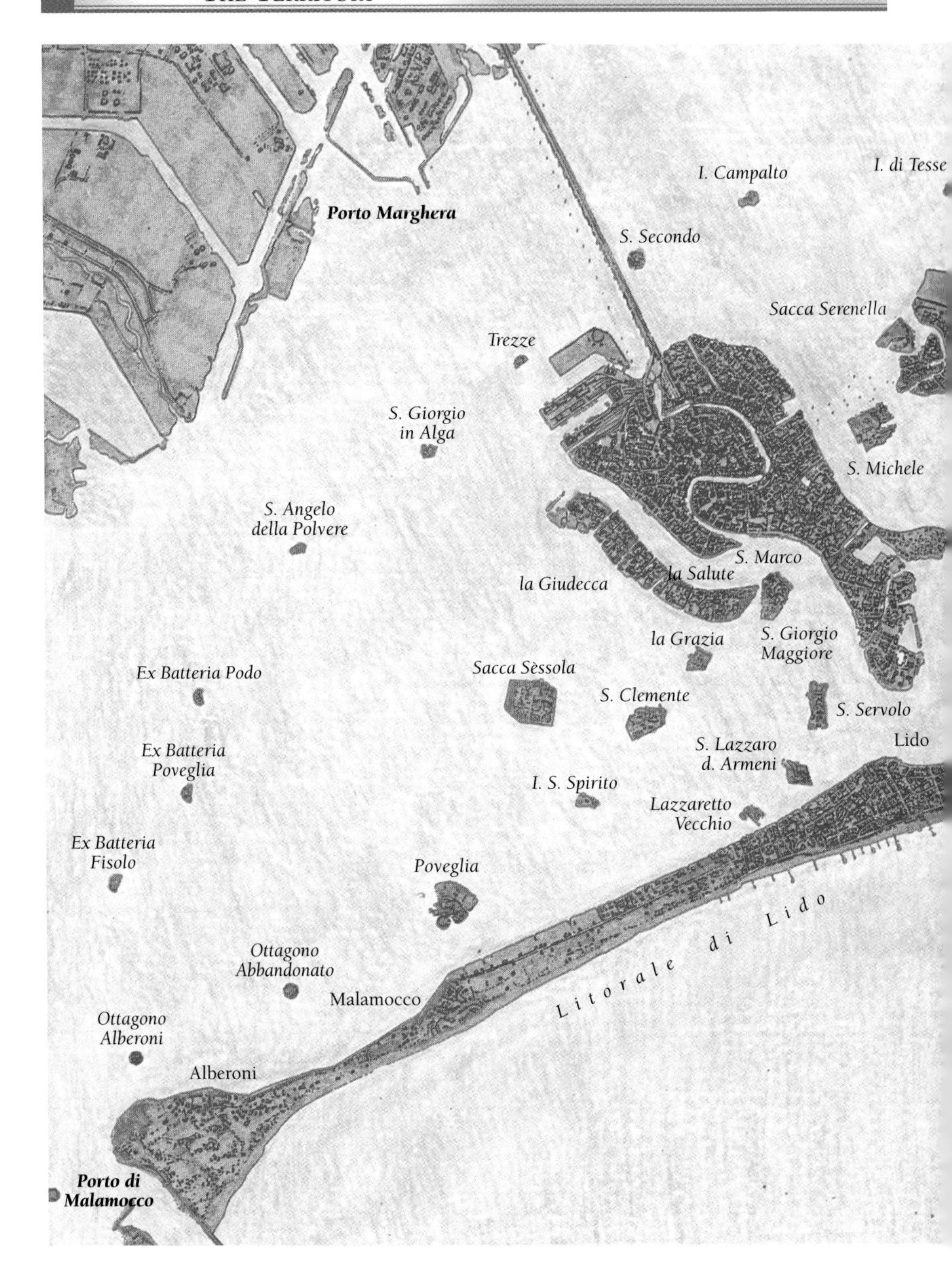
Porto Marghera
I. Campalto
I. di Tesse
S. Secondo
Sacca Serenella
Trezze
S. Giorgio
in Alga
S. Michele
S. Angelo
della Polvere
S. Marco
la Salute
la Giudecca
la Grazia
S. Giorgio
Maggiore
Sacca Sèssola
Ex Batteria Podo
S. Clemente
S. Servolo
Lido
Ex Batteria
Poveglia
S. Lazzaro
d. Armeni
I. S. Spirito
Lazzaretto
Vecchio
Ex Batteria
Fisolo
Poveglia
Litorale di Lido
Ottagono
Abbandonato
Malamocco
Ottagono
Alberoni
Alberoni
Porto di
Malamocco

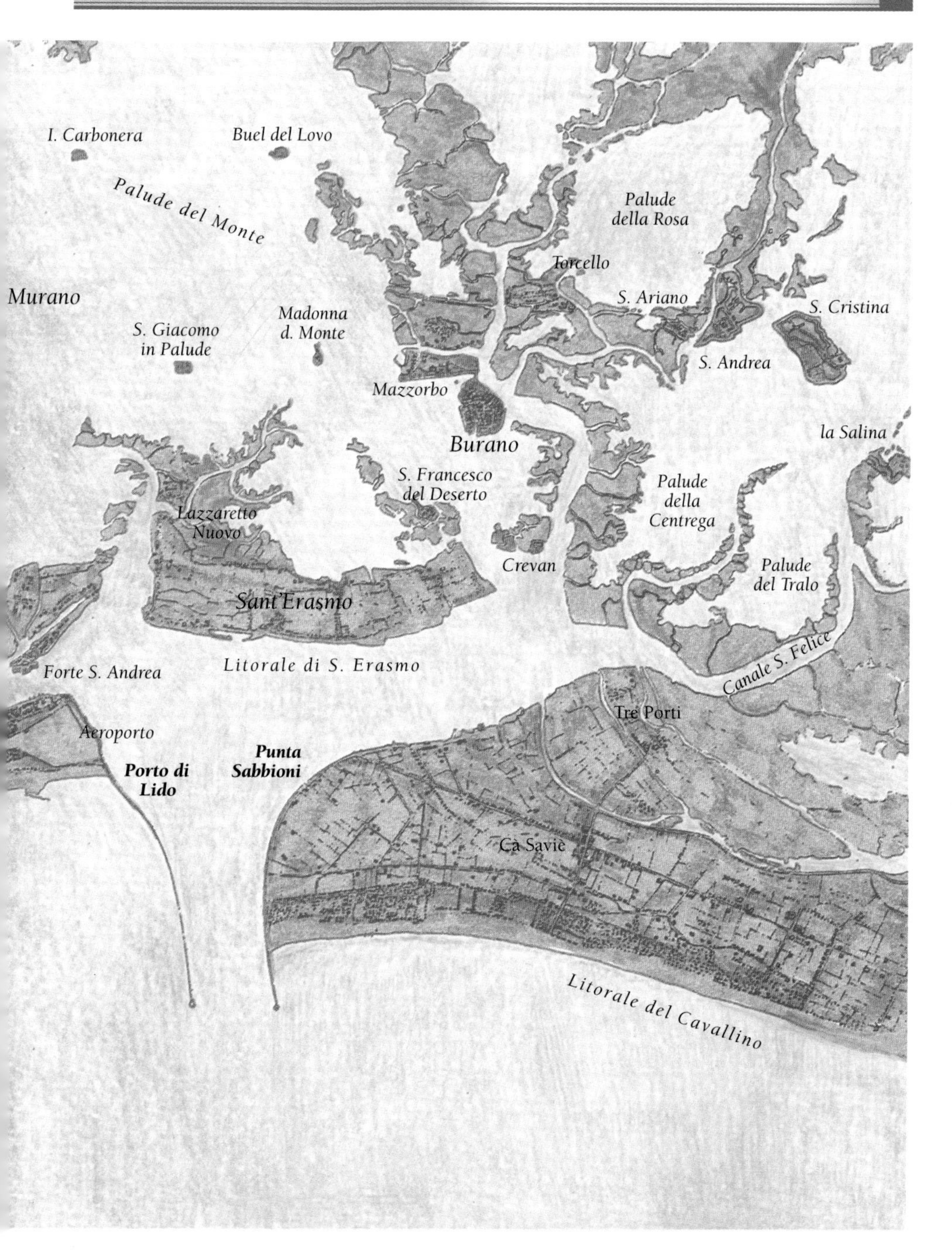
I. Carbonera
Buel del Lovo
Palude del Monte
Palude della Rosa
Torcello
Murano
S. Giacomo in Palude
Madonna d. Monte
S. Ariano
S. Cristina
S. Andrea
Mazzorbo
Burano
la Salina
S. Francesco del Deserto
Palude della Centrega
Lazzaretto Nuovo
Crevan
Palude del Tralo
Sant'Erasmo
Canale S. Felice
Forte S. Andrea
Litorale di S. Erasmo
Tre Porti
Aeroporto
Punta Sabbioni
Porto di Lido
Cà Saviè
Litorale del Cavallino

The Origins Of The Legend

To be sure, the history of Venice finds its origins in the mists of time, when, more than one thousand five hundred years before Christ, **Neolithic populations** left the mountains of TRENTINO and the EUGANEAN HILLS and dedicated themselves to **the reclamation of this marshy zone** in VENETO. The inhabitants built their dwellings atop long wooden stilts which were sunk into the muddy ground. They also **constructed their pile houses along the tranquil lagoon**, far from the communication routes of the mainland, and exploited the natural resources available in order to survive.

Titus Livius, the great Roman historian, describes a ***violent clash***, which took place in the fourth century BC, between some ***lagoon dwellers*** – easily identifiable as those from Venice – and the ***warriors of Cleomenes of Sparta***. The warriors, it seems, were recalled by Cleomenes, but not without having to leave behind some of their boats in the retreat. And, even if his story does sound a bit like a legend, it is undeniable that **small communities** of farmers and fishermen, who were isolated from the surrounding territory, **lived** in this area **for many years**.

During the period of Roman domination (at which time the inhabitants were immediately granted Roman citizenship),

Torcello, in the vicinity of Altino, it was one of the first islands to receive "refugees" from the mainland.

A "casone", traditional dwelling of the original settlers of the lagoon.

though many inland cities such as VERONA, VICENZA, ESTE, TREVISO, AQUILEIA, CIVIDALE DEL FRIULI and UDINE were founded and developed, there was no lack of communities along the coast: ADRIA, ODERZO and ALTINO, are to name a few.

The lagoons probably supplied the inhabitants of this last community (situated near today's Marco Polo Airport and known for its beautiful woods, its clear water and its villas), with delicious seafood, fish, garden produce and salt.

Existence was not easy in those centuries, but it was certainly tranquil. They lived on the boundary of the port activity of CHIOGGIA which controlled all direct traffic to PADUA and in which lived many salt-workers and tax collectors. They were also near to *Equilus* (JESOLO) and the LITORALE DEL CAVALLINO where they had settlements of skilled horse and cattle breeders. This was the situation, at least until hostile populations from distant lands arrived who, through a series of tragic events (in addition to continual conflicts between emperors and pretenders to the throne), defined the **crisis and the end of the Western Roman Empire.**

Certainly, in the course of those **difficult years**, marked also by particularly wet and cold periods and by continual famine and pestilence, **many people looked for refuge in the tranquil waters of the lagoon**, far away from the dangerous raids made by the enemies of the *Pax Romana*.

In 410, **Alaric, the king of the Visigoths**, reached as far as ROME, and then plundered it. Shortly after this, on **the 25th of March, 421**, if one is to believe the legendary date of the birth of Venice, a group of "refugees" occupied some small islands that were situated along the course of a *rivus altus* (Rialto) – a deep canal that crossed the lagoon.

Thirty years later, in 421, **Attila the Hun** invaded the peninsula and plundered not only AQUILEIA, but also ALTINO, provoking a second migration of "refugees" and, according to the legend, giving birth to the **political unity of Venice.**

It is certain that, after the end of **the Western Roman Empire** (476 AD), when **Theodoric, king of the Ostrogoths, came to Italy** (with the consensus of Zeno, the emperor of the Eastern Roman Empire) and established the capital of his kingdom in RAVENNA, there was already a stable and well organized population living in the Venetian lagoon. It is documented, by the numerous writings of **Cassiodorus** (Roman minister of the "barbarous" king), that Theodoric demanded tribute from the inhabitants of the region, as

A mosaic, in the Byzantine style, in the basilica at Torcello, founded in 693, readapted later on.

would have befitted anyone who was a real member of the kingdom.

Cassiodorus admirably describes the life of the people who inhabited the lagoon. Already then it was considered a **"unique" place** where rich and poor lived together, where the common currency was salt, where pontoons went up and down the canals, pulled along by men walking the tow-paths among beds of reeds and vegetable gardens, where there were boats rather than horses hitched alongside the houses, where the high and low tides played water games with the shoreline – at first shallow, then deep.

After **the death of Theodoric**, other **Emperors of the Easr** came to Italy, and the lagoons became a part of the **Byzantine Exarchate of Ravenna**. Again, the legend claims that, for the assistance granted by the Venetians against the Goths and the Franks, the ***Byzantines granted autonomy to the islands of Rialto***, inspiring them to construct the churches of **San Teodoro** and **San Giminiano.**

Among the various activities of the lagoon, one of the most important from the start was the care of vegetable gardens.

Nevertheless, another "barbarous" people, the **Lombards,** were about to arrive in Italy. Little by little they had begun **to occupy the hinterlands of Veneto**, robbing the most important cities from the Byzantines, but not managing to invade the lagoon zone where new refugees poured in, bringing with them the desire to defend themselves from the fury of the invaders. Among them were **churchmen, soldiers, families and rich landowners**.

The increased population made it necessary to reclaim new land for agriculture; to consolidate the banks with a fixed foundation of stilts which were embedded into the sea bed; to dig canals in order to maintain contact with the sea; and to deal with the tides.

According to some, **the second act of the birth of Venice** began in this way in 640. A new city, CITTANOVA, was founded in the middle of the lagoon. Nothing remains of this city except, according to some scholars, a stone found at the foundations of the **Cathedral of Torcello**. And it was here that, according to legend, twelve noble families elected **Paoloccio Anafesto**, their **first doge,** about sixty years after the city's founding.

The Origins Of The Written History

According to legend, the Venetian lagoon system was created as a shelter for refugees coming from the inland of Veneto during the turbulent events that struck the Italian peninsula in the dark centuries. Every legend has its roots in historical characters, and certainly no scholar could deny the authenticity of a development of a nucleus in the lagoon which, step by step, became larger and more organized, and which must have begun precisely in those centuries. **The autonomous organization of Venice** was, instead, a subsequent event – if one gives credit to the testimony of commentators of the period who saw the events take place in person, and witnessed the protagonists themselves: the **Byzantines,** the **Lombards** and the **Franks.**

In 527, **Justinian** took the throne of the Eastern Roman Empire. Thirteen years later, his general, **Belisarius**, overtook the Italian peninsula by conquering RAVENNA. This became the **seat of power of the Byzantine Exarchate in Italy.** The inhabitants of the lagoon, subjects to Byzantium, weren't particularly numerous at the time, but, in the years

The church of the Holy Wisdom in Constantinople, built by Justinian. The minarets were added afterwards by Muslims.

that followed, when the Lombards began their penetration, the population notably increased. The cities of Veneto were occupied and fell to ruin one after another. Meanwhile, there was a dramatic development in the lagoon under the military government of the m*agister militum* of ISTRIA who was a direct representative of the Exarchate of Ravenna.

In that period, the second half of the 7th century, the civilian administration was led by governors of the major islands – the *tribunes*. In the same year, CITTANOVA was founded in the center of the lagoon. Meanwhile, the **clashes between the Byzantines and the Lombards** were becoming more and more dramatic. At the end of the 7th century, the *tribunes* and the *magister militium* left the post to a *dux* – a doge recognized by the Byzantine government. **The first doge** of Venice, according to some historians, was Paulicio. He was elected, according to the words of a commentator named **Giovanni Diacono**, in 697, or, according to the *Cronicon Altinate* between 713 and 715. Other sources sustain that the first doge was **Orso Ipato**, elected in 727 after the conclusion of a military revolt which ended tragically with the killing of the exarch of Ravenna.

Emperor Constantine IX in a mosaic from the church of the Holy Wisdom in Constantinople.

They were difficult years but rich with dramatic events. In 740, **Liutprand**, king of the Lombards, conquered RAVENNA. The exarch took refuge in the lagoons of Veneto and was eventually able to recapture his city, with the help of the Venetians, the year after. The Venetians were granted even more autonomy as a result of their fidelity and aid in this conquest.

In 751, the Lombards definitively conquered Ravenna, but by then, Venice had transferred its seat of power to MALAMOCCO, at the southern heights of the shores of Lido. Venice was now an entity completely independent.

In 754, the Pope solicited the help of the Franks to fight against the power of the Lombards in Italy. In 756, **Astolfus**, king of the Lombards, was forced to surrender to **Pippin**, king of the Franks and exarch of Ravenna (as far as the mouth of the Po river). Between 764 and 765, an assembly consisting of all the representatives of the community elected **doge Maurizio Galbaio**. A glorious history had begun for Venice.

Birth Of A Republic

In 774, **Charles, the king of the Franks** (and future emperor) **defeated, the Lombards once and for all.** In the same year, **he gave the exarchate of Ravenna, Venice and Istria to Pope Adrian**, increasing the hostility of the Byzantines. Four years later, the Christmas night of the eight hundred, in ROME, Charles was crowned by the Pope as emperor of the Holy Roman Empire.

The Eastern Empire (by now incapable of controlling the peninsula) and **the Empire of Charlemagne** fought at length for the possession of Venice. There were also diverse factions of the city (developed in part on the mainland and in part in the lagoon) which participated in this conflict.

After a series of events, **Pippin**, Charlemagne's son, went to Venice with his army to conquer the lagoon (810), but by then, the inhabitants of the islands were able to push him back. Charlemagne and the emperor of Byzantium, **Nice-**

forus, worked out an **agreement** (the *Pax Nicefori*), somewhere between 811 and 814, which stated **that the city was to be assigned to the Eastern Empire once and for all.**

At the end of this tragic conflict, which could have transformed Venice into a stronghold of the Holy Roman Empire, the city's government was transferred from Malamocco to the islands of the *rivus altus* – **Rialto**. Here the center of the lagoon was well protected and had a great influx of people coming from other localities closer to the shores or from the mainland. Now Venice would be unable to continue with its **sea-faring trade** or to strengthen its **ties with the Orient** through the development of new routes towards Byzantium.

The Lion of San Marco in two different representations. On the adjoining page: *a sculpture from the 11th century;* above: *the lion that, according to legend, was brought to Venice together with the remains of the saint, becoming the symbol of the Serenissima, and that still stands today in Piazza Ducale.*

In 828, the city witnessed an **extraordinary event** which was symbolic of its ties with the eastern shores of the Mediterranean. From Alexandria, in Egypt, **the body of Saint Mark the Evangelist was moved to Venice**. For this reason, it was decided to build a basilica which would bear his name.

The event, however, is **immured in legend**: it seems that two Venetian merchants, Rustico da Torcello and Bon da Malamocco, decided to rescue the sacred body from those who were not able to honor it properly. With the help of a priest, they stole it and covered it with pig's flesh – so as to get it passed the Arab customs officials who considered such meat foul. After having miraculously escaped to the sea, a terrible storm broke and the two were forced to land in Venice. They were greeted by a festive crowd who were awaiting the Patriarch of GRADO and the doge **Giustiniano.** The sweet scent of roses permeated the canals and the islands. In order to conserve the remains in a dignified manner, **Giustiniano arranged for the construction of a church** next to the dogal palace that would become the Church of the State.

In 840, another, perhaps less evocative but certainly important, event took place which marked another stage in the history of the independence of Venice. The Doge **Pietro Tradonico** signed an agreement called the ***Pactum Lotharii*** with **Lothair** – the emperor of the Holy Roman Empire. It dealt with an updated version of the agreement that Charles and Niceforus (the two emperors who had once challenged each other for control of the lagoon) had signed thirty years earlier. Now the doge would not only be recognized by the title of **glorious Duke of Venice,** but he would also be given the possibility to coordinate the alliance with the Eastern Empire on his own behalf.

The ***Pactum Lotharii*** was a very important document which clarified the dimensions of the Duke of Venice's possessions in those years. The duke possessed **seventeen settlements** whose borders touched those of GRADO, to the northeast, and CAVARZERE, to the southwest, as well as thirteen of the islands which were near to the Grand Canal, Murano and Torcello. Venice, therefore, controlled all of the lagoon and was ready to **amplify its dominions to the south, towards Comacchio** (a dangerous competitor in the salt trade which was attacked and destroyed by the Venetians in 833) and towards the **Slavic territory** on the coast of ISTRIA and DALMATIA. It was also able **to defend itself against the Hungarians** who were coming down through the peninsula to make war, but who were eventually defeated near Albiola in 899.

To better understand how one lived and what the most important economical activities were in those days, it is a good

One of the most important Venetian activities was the building of ships, which gave work to a large number of local artisans.

idea to refer to the writings of **Giovanni Diacono,** the commentator from Veneto and the author of a history of Venice (*Chronicon venetum*), from its origins, until 1008 and the Annals of Fulda.

Along with the numbers of **fishermen, salt-workers, farmers, produce dealers, and landowners,** the numbers of **sailors** and **merchants** increased. **The glass industry** had already begun to make its appearance in the lagoon and was manufacturing products that were sold along the coast of the Adriatic. As early as the 9th century, trade relations with countries beyond the Alps had begun, and even the nobles, who had always detested business activities, began to foresee the possibility of investing their assets in the **maritime trades.** These trades were tied to salt and spices and slaves. In his will, Doge **Giustiniano Partecipazio** named a fond of one thousand two hundred lira to be invested in the maritime trade. In the same way, **Orso**, another doge from the same family, cites pepper, which later became one of the most important spices to be traded between the Orient and the West.

Traffic along the rivers, along the **Adige** to VERONA, for example, or along the **Po** up to LOMBARDY, procured trade relations throughout all of northern Italy. The Venetian fleet became a major player in the exchange between the Orient and Europe as early as the beginning of the 10th century.

Liutprand from Cremona, who went to BYZANTIUM as a delegate of Emperor **Otto II**, told of the Venetians skill for the smuggling purple cloth and silk whose exportation was against the laws of the empire. On their way towards the Orient, merchants carried metals, slaves and timber and on their return they carried spices and cloth. In those years an animosity against the Slavic populations was born, which would last for centuries. Under Doge Pietro Orseolo, around 1000, the Venetian expansion in Dalmatia began. While in 1082, for its assistance in the conflict against the Normans, Venice received from Byzantium complete **tax exemption** for trade throughout all of the empire, and, in Byzantium, it obtained three stockyards and a series of warehouses located in strategic points. AMALFI, which, until that moment had been a major protagonist at sea, was surpassed by Venice which began to have a leading role, even in respect to Genoa and Pisa.

At The Threshold Of 1000

Between the 8th and 11th centuries, **Venice evolved**, strengthening its ties with the Orient and becoming one of the most powerful sea-faring cities on the Mediterranean. Inevitably, there were reasons for envy and jealousy among the other cities. GENOA and PISA, for example, tried in every way to impose their own supremacy – though without success.

In 1096, as a result of religious, political and social demands of the time and following the oppressive behavior of the Turks in respect to the Christian pilgrims who were gathering in Palestine, **Pope Urban II declared the first crusade**. This meant out and out war, the objective of which was to liberate the Holy Sepulcher from the infidels.

In this way, a series of expeditions (led by landowners, kings and emperors) begun. These expeditions managed, at least initially, to win over the city of Jerusalem. This determined the expansion of European possession in the surrounding territory and it **enormously improved relations, both commercial and otherwise, between the West and the Orient.**

The church of the Holy Sepulcher in Jerusalem. Its liberation was the object of the Crusades.

PISA, GENOA and VENICE, who couldn't help but be involved in this situation, now had even more reason to clash and to increase their rivalries.

In 1098, PISA, on its way to the shores of Syria with its fleet, had devastated the Ionic islands which were controlled by the Byzantines. VENICE, which, thanks to Byzantium, enjoyed commercial privileges with these islands, decided to intervene in order to protect its interests. In 1099, a **Venetian fleet**, on its way to Palestine, stopped near RHODES and **overcame the Pisan fleet.** The Pisans were forced to abandon trade pursuits in Byzantine ports, leaving the monopoly to the Venetians.

The Venetian fleet continued towards the Palestinian coast, contributing to the conquest of

Haifa. It was not, however, able to obtain the same brilliant results that Genoa had obtained. And, in the following years, Venice was not able to keep up with its rival. This is because, **beyond subjugating lands in Dalmatia and Istria,** it had **to protect the privileges it had obtained from Byzantium** (those that the emperor would have liked to reduce, by the way). In reality, Byzantium depended entirely on Venice, both for its economy and its safety, even though, from a territorial point of view, Venice had not expanded its land holdings beyond the borders that it had achieved in the 9th century.

Beyond the dogal palace and the church of San Marco (which was built after the basilica of the Twelve Holy Apostles in Byzantium) the lagoon city now hosted some seventy churches (San Giovanni Decollato was erected in 1007). Its appearance was gradually being modified: many islands on the periphery had been abandoned; the Rialto area had undergone an intense reclamation in order to make room for those who wished to live in the heart of the city; and there were numerous brick buildings which had sprung up beside those still made of wood. The doge was looking more and more like a prince – especially to the world outside of Venice.

The routes of the crusaders toward the Holy Land in the outlawed expedition of Urban II (1096-1099).

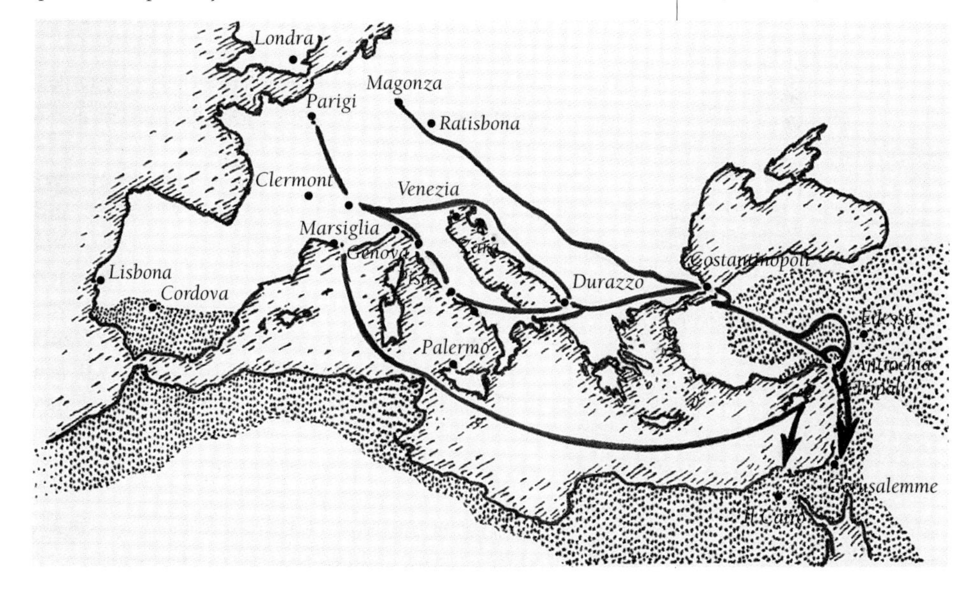

Between The Pope And The Emperor

While Venice was consolidating its role as the bridge between the East and the West, and developing more intense commercial traffic, **the feudal world** in Italy (locked inside the castles of the vassals of the Holy Germanic Roman Empire) **had broken apart**, opening itself up to a civic order which had a new player – the middle class.

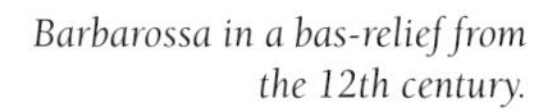

Barbarossa in a bas-relief from the 12th century.

The cities had been repopulated and **had developed self-sufficient organizing skills.** They were far from the bonds of obedience once imposed upon them by the sovereign monarchs of the proceeding centuries (although the rivalry between the principal centers and the smaller ones was still strong). **Imperial authority** (at that moment, far away from the peninsula, and busy on other fronts, while the birth of the independent communities was changing the structure of Italy) **was once again becoming arrogant enough to demand its rights**, and was being requested everywhere – especially by the communities which felt weakest. **Frederick I**, called **Barbarossa** (Red Beard), from the house of Hohenstaufen, took the throne in 1152 **hoping to extend his dominion throughout the entire peninsula**. He had sent his armies out many times and was finally able to destroy MILAN.

Venice, who was earning considerable profits from its trade activities in the north of the peninsula and on the other side of the Alps, **was no stranger to this conflict.** It had begun in the middle of the 12th century and finished only after thirty years of fighting when the autonomy of the communes was recognized in **Constance's Peace Treaty** of 1183. But Venice's main role was to act as mediator between the pope (who supported the communes as opposed to the mega-power of the imperial authority) and the emperor.

In 1167, Venice **became a member of the league**

of Lombard Communes whose mandate was signed at **Pontida**. But its struggle against Barbarossa was more economical in nature than military. In 1172, in order to safeguard its relationship with Byzantium during that stormy period, Venice supported the emperor in his conflict against Ancona. In order to stay on the good side of Pope Alexander III, it hosted and protected the cardinals that he supported and who were against the anti-pope – then under the protection of Barbarossa.

In short, **Venice tried to make itself the hatchet of everyone**. On the 24th of July, 1177, the city assisted in the peacemaking coronation of Alexander III and Frederick I in which the king of Sicily, princes, landowners, and civil and religious leaders from the entire peninsula participated.

The **meeting** was so **solemn** and important that **many legends have been built-up** around it. One of these was that the pope bestowed the insignia of the Serenissima (the **honorary chair**, the **cushion**, the **candle**, the **naked sword** and the **silver tomb**) upon the doge who held it until its fall. These were in reality the symbols of Byzantine authority and therefore must have predated those years. The celebration of the Wedding of the Sea, whose origins date back to before that historic encounter, was probably exchanged for the Festival of the Ascension which is still being celebrated today.

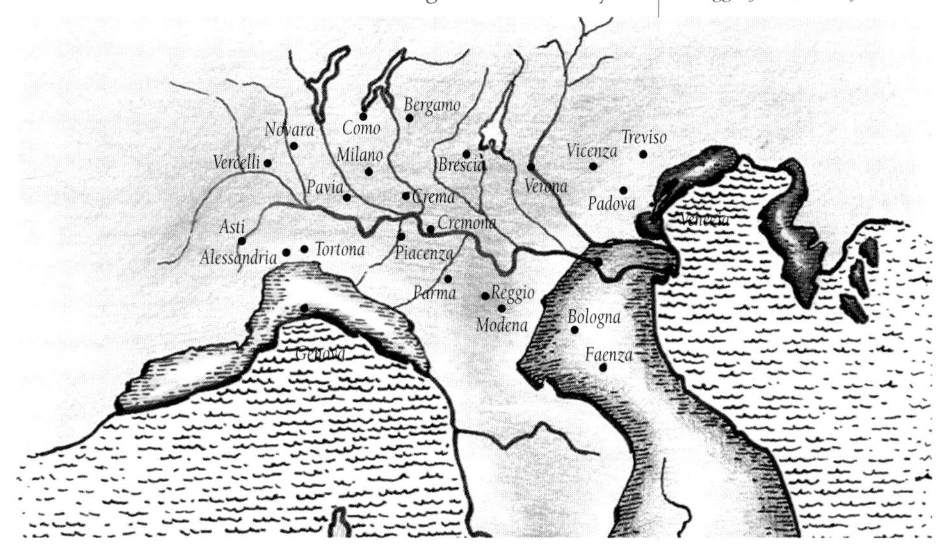

Italian communities in a struggle for autonomy.

The Conquest Of The Mediterranean

Its trade relations with the Eastern Empire, its ability as a negotiator between the East and the West, and the its contrast between the Christian and the Muslim worlds (which became an open conflict with the beginning of the crusades), all contributed to the increase of Venice's prestige and power.

That power could never be exercised, however, because there were other republics, in particular PISA and GENOA, who wished to control the Mediterranean Sea. Their commercial trade took place mostly in the **Tyrrhenian Sea** (to the detriment of the Muslims whose fleets the two republics had fought against for many years – often together). **Pisa had been plundered** twice, in 1004 and in 1011, but **at the end of the 11th century the Tyrrhenian Sea was under its control**. Sardinia and Corsica had been wrested from the Muslims repeatedly in 1022 and in 1091, and the coasts of **Egypt, Tunisia and Spain** were by now habitual **landing places for the Pisan and Genoese merchant vessels.** In 1097, during the first of the Crusades, Genoa and Pisa established bases in Syria and Palestine. **Pisa**, in **1111**, and **Genoa**, in **1142,** obtained their own headquarters in **Constantinople**, where Venice had already been settled for some years.

A miniature based on Digenis Akritas, *the Byzantine poem that tells of the commander of an oriental garrison posted to defend against the infidel.*

Collaborating with both Baldwin I and Baldwin II, kings of Jerusalem, **Venice** had obtained notable **commercial privileges** in the HOLY LAND. Relations between Venice and the Eastern Empire, though contradictory and marked by moments of disagreement, nevertheless permitted the city to carry forward its own commercial interests. The volume of business among the three republics was growing enormously and each aspired to maintain itself on the traffic of the other two.

A "solido", the coin of the Byzantine Empire.

In 1171, **Manuele I Comnenus**, the emperor of the East, **expelled** the **Venetian merchants** from Constantinople, and the empire's trade was entrusted to Genoa and Pisa. A few years afterward, the **Byzantines**, who had been able to subdue the Christian rule in Palestine, **were conquered by the Turks in the battle of Myriokephalon** (1176). This was the beginning of Venice's good fortune.

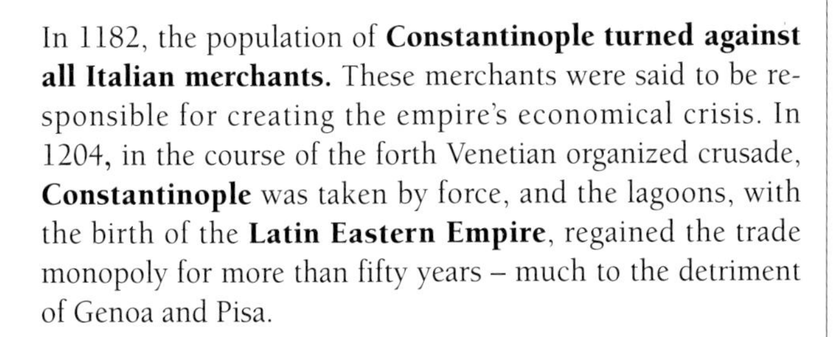

In 1182, the population of **Constantinople turned against all Italian merchants.** These merchants were said to be responsible for creating the empire's economical crisis. In 1204, in the course of the forth Venetian organized crusade, **Constantinople** was taken by force, and the lagoons, with the birth of the **Latin Eastern Empire**, regained the trade monopoly for more than fifty years – much to the detriment of Genoa and Pisa.

These were **intense years**, in the course of which, according to some historians, **Venice** became so **powerful** that there was a **proposal**, which failed by only one vote, ***to transfer the capital of Venice to Constantinople.* Its control of the Mediterranean increased.** Firm agreements were made with the Sultan of EGYPT and with ARMENIA; CORFU was occupied; and CRETE, which would be ruled by the Venetians for five centuries, was conquered and numerous Venetian colonies were transferred there._

In 1261, the year of the collapse of the Eastern Latin Empire, **Nicolò** and **Maffio Polo**, two rich Venetian merchants, **set off for their first voyage in Cathay.**

Venice In The 13th Century

It was the 9th of May, 1204 and Venice, along with its Doge **Enrico Dandolo**, seized the capital of the Eastern Empire - Constantinople. **Baldwin of Flanders** (after being elected by five bishops, an abbot and six noble Venetians, who were given a quarter of the Byzantine territory including its capital, the coasts of ANATOLIA and the ISLANDS OF THE AEGEAN SEA) **then became sovereign of the *new* Eastern Latin Empire**. **Bonifacio di Monferrato and the barons of the Crusades** received a part of the GREEK TERRITORIES.

All lands that could guarantee the safety of sea traffic were given to Venice: EPIRUS and the islands of the IONIAN SEA, ACARNANIA and AETOLIA, a good part of PELOPONNESUS, the islands of AEGINA and SALAMIS, some fortresses in EUBOEA, the CYCLADES, ADRIANOPLE, the coasts of MARMARA, etc. The doge was given the title of "**Ruler of a quarter part and half of all the Empire of Romania**", a pompous sounding title, but it testified to the level to which the lagoon city had reached.

The transportation of wool in a miniature from the 13th century.

How did the city of the 13th century present itself – while its men were conquering the seas and while the Polos were reaching the far away lands of CATHAY? The lagoon borders were more or less unchanged in respect to the past, but foreign visitor could not help but be struck by the richness and vitality of Venice in those days.

The **Rialto port of call** became an arrival and departure point for a commercial traffic that was so highly developed that it directly interested the entire population of the city. The laws of the republic prohibited ship owners and merchants to make direct contact with other ports along the Adriatic coast, which were anyway under Venetian control.

At **Rialto** – crossroads of the world – the fruit and vegetable **markets**, as well as the dairy and fish **markets** were particularly busy. **Nu-**

A big mask placed outside a rope factory; hemp rope come out of its mouth.

merous hotels, often managed by religious corporations or aristocratic families, began springing up. **State offices**, in which the magistrates who dealt with customs and property taxes worked, were also involved. Often citizens were asked personal loans to finance the military.

Foreign businessmen came to the city for their interests not only in **import products** like silk and spices, but also in **products made locally** like **wool fabric** and **leather** (localized primarily at Giudecca); **glassware** (mostly transferred to MURANO to avoid danger of fires); **ships** at the state shipyards; products for the manufacture of **hemp ropes**, indispensable for navigation.

Near to San Marco, there were the ***Frezzeria*** and the ***Spaderia***, the streets in which arrows and swords were fabricated. There were the *rughe* (streets) dedicated to the **goldsmiths** as well as to other craftsmen. The **Milanese** had their neighborhoods there; also **those from the mainland of Veneto**; the **Istrians**; the **Dalmatians**; and those from the regions of **Romagna**, **Emilia**, **Marche**, **Abruzzo** and **Apuglia**; the **Florentines** and **those from Lucca**. There was no lack of foreigners – **Greeks**, **Albanians**, and **French**, but overall **Germans** who had their own *fondaco* or quarter. **Jews** were initially located at Giudecca, but were eventually expelled to MESTRE before being transferred to the *Ghetto* after a council had decided to isolate them from the Christians.

Doctors created a professional association in 1258, and their statutes prohibited them from receiving kick-backs from the pharmacists for the medicine they had prescribed. The **pharmacists**, on the other hand, were prohibited from selling medicine without a prescription. The **state issued a declaration** which obliged all doctors, no matter how eminent, to give their services to the poor without charge.

Furthermore, the **state controlled prices on foodstuffs** and dealt with the storage of goods which were to be put on

The golden horses in Piazza San Marco are the work of a Greek from the 3rd century BC. The Doge Enrico Dondolo brought them to Venice in 1204 when Constantinople was taken by force during the fourth Crusade.

the market in case of scarcity or famine. The state also issued a limit, in the 13th century, for the number of months an accused person could remain in jail before trail.

Next to the oldest church of Venice arose other bigger ones dedicated to **Saints John and Paul and Santa Maria Gloriosa dei Frari.**

Saint Mark's Square was judged "the most beautiful square in the world" by foreign visitors; **the Dogal Palace** was a "grand and beautiful wonder".

Common people, sailors, merchants and gentlemen alike mixed freely in the streets of the city, and in their midst, the togas of the **numerous magistrates** of the city could be clearly distinguished. The most elegant among these magistrates were those who represented the Major Council. **Religious festivals, like Easter and Christmas, were occasions for magnificent ceremonies** which brought people from distant lands and so added to the fascination and the prestige of the city.

In short, Venice in the 13th century was a booming city, prosperous, busy with economic activities, and administered by an intelligent and energetic ruling class. Political life was dominated by **the presence of the doges**, assisted by dignitaries, chosen on the bases of their competence, and supported by the bishops whose power was gradually diminishing.

The office of the **doge, which had initially been elected** (since an assembly of citizens, called **arengo** or **concio**, had called for him to proclaim it as such), became, with the passing of time, an inherited position (although informally so). In reality, the noble families had control of the actions of the doges and subjected them to many restraints.

In 1143, the **Council of the Wise** appeared and the only duty of the assembly of citizens was to ratify the decisions they made. In 1172, this council took on the name of **Maggior Consiglio** (Major Council) and was supported by a **Minor Consiglio** (Minor Council) composed of the Doge's advisors. Between 1207 and 1212 the **Quarantia** was created, and in 1255, the **Consiglio dei Rogati** – a very particular assembly of citizens – came to life. This assembly was initially composed of sixty members. The number of participants in political life was therefore dramatically elevated. In 1297 the lockout of the Major Council brought the number of the general assembly to nearly one thousand, but every seat – instead of being elected – was inherited.

Venice as seen from above. In the foreground, the Dogana da Mar which once acted as docking for boats arriving from the Orient.

Beyond The Mediterranean

Niccolò and **Maffio Polo**, the Venetian merchants who had business in Constantinople, transferred their businesses to the Black Sea at Soldaia after the collapse of the Eastern Latin Empire. From there, in 1261, they set out for **a business voyage towards Cathay**, following an unusual route for that time. They crossed PERSIA and CENTRAL ASIA and arrived at the courts of **Kublai Khan**, the lord of all Tartars. **After eight years they returned home** with an embassy for the pope. They remained in Venice only two years – enough time to have an answer from the pontiff Gregory X to bring to Kublai Khan. **In 1271, they left again, this time with young Marco, Niccolò's son, for a voyage that would last twenty years.**

On the way, they crossed PERSIA, the desert region of KHORASAN (in the direction of BADAKHSHAN and PAMIR), and the great desert of GOBI. Then they descended into the regions of Chinese TURKESTAN and MONGOLIA and went as far as CHEMENFU, where, in 1275, they met Kublai Khan. KAMBALUC – today's PEKING and KINSAI – today's HANG-CHOW (at that time the ancient capital of the Sung Empire) were a few of the places that the Polos had the possibility to visit and collect information. Finally, in **1291**, in order to accompany **Princess Cocacin**, the betrothed of a Persian sovereign, **the Polos had the possibility to return to Venice**. This time they traveled over the ocean rather than the sea. The **log of the miracu-**

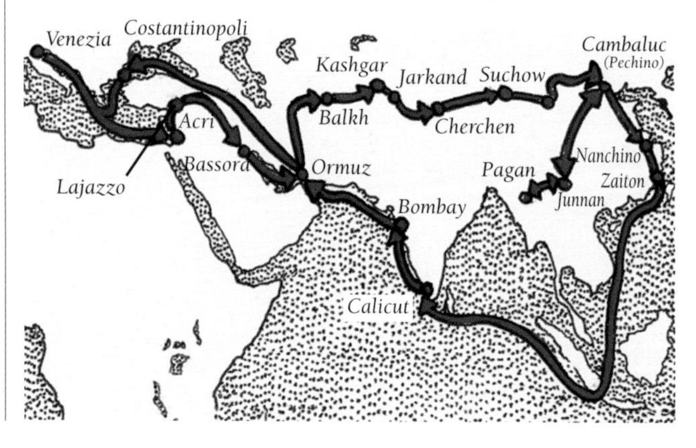

The voyage of Marco Polo who stayed away from Venice for twenty-five years.

lous exploits of that long voyage were compiled during a difficult period in which, in September 1268, Marco was taken prisoner during the **battle of Curzola** (between the Genoese and the Venetians). In prison, a companion of misfortune, **Rustichello of Pisa**, collected and transcribed the stories, entitled ***Il Milione***, that amazed innumerable readers.

Legend has it that upon their return in 1295, the Polos knocked on the front door of their house and were asked by the servant: *Chi xe?* (Who is it?) to which they had simply replied: "It's us, the owners", as if to say that twenty-five years of absence didn't represent anything extraordinary. ***The behavior of the Polos*** was certainly romanticized, but it was nevertheless ***emblematic of the conditions of the lives of the merchants and their families.***

Title page of the first edition of "Il Milione" *by Marco Polo.*

The **young son** of any Venetian merchant was **destined to study** under the guide of a teacher of grammar and arithmetic. Then, **at fourteen, he was placed on a merchant vessel** as a crossbowman to sail through the Mediterranean. Here he learned about the difficult life of a sailor and had the opportunity to organize a little of his own commerce. **After some years at sea, the father or relative of the young man, placed him on a** family vessel where he learned about the merchant's trade. **This was followed by years of experience in a distant port of call which was under family control. Only at a mature age could the merchant be allowed to return to Venice and establish himself.** There he could entrust the distant company to a son or a nephew and finally occupy himself, in first person, with public life.

Along this path, **the women**, who usually married very young, spent their lives in waiting – raising children (destined to leave at a very young age) and putting up with the moderation of her elders. A famous scholar of the time stated that: "The greatness of Venice is also due, in part, to the stoicism and sacrifices suffered by its women."

Between Land And Sea

The battle of Meloria, a decisive moment for the fate of Pisa who was defeated by Genoa.

From 1379 to 1380, in order to collect the funds necessary to sustain the warlike expenses in Venice, a **general valuation** was compiled. In the six sectors of the city, a census found **two thousand families** with an income higher than the minimum taxable amount. **Half of the families in this group were noble families. Others included: wholesaler merchants, shipbuilders, spice dealers, haberdashers, rag dealers, fabric retailers, cheese sellers and craftsmen** of every type (as, for example, masons or dyers).

There were numerous **families with lower incomes** as well. Among these were, **many noble families who had lost their fortunes** and to whom the state often granted the possibility to trade in pepper.

Venice of the 13th century was a **great metropolis** in which a large number of people were residents and a larger number came and went. Although there were many problems tied to that period, ***life in Venice remained relatively tranquil***, without conflicts between the "popolo minuto" who had lost all of their "political" prerogatives and the "popolo grasso" who had control of the public domain.

In the month of June, 1310, **the Council of the Ten was formed**. This council became a permanent fixture twenty-five years later and had the tasks of preparing the trails of those who had conspired against the Republic and watching over its security.

In the first half of the century, Venice didn't have privileged relations with Constantinople. They turned their attention instead to the southeastern area of the Mediterranean and were active in strengthening **trade with the Muslims in Egypt**

and in Syria, even though this was forbidden by the Pope. The two countries were, in fact, important geographical points of reference for caravans traveling into Africa, and obligatory passageways for goods coming from the Far East and India and from across the Gulf of Oman and the Red Sea.

While Venice had become master of the sea, there were, on the peninsula, numerous seignories in conflict over control of the land. So Venice turned **its attention to the peninsula**, allying itself with Florence, Milan, Ferrara and with **Charles of Luxembourg** in the **Florentine-Milanese League** which was heading towards war with Verona. Verona was guilty of extending its dominion to the borders of the lagoons. In 1337, it obtained Treviso, Ceneda and Castelfranco from **Mastino II della Scala**. These were the first Venetian territories on dry ground.

In 1348, like the rest of Europe, Venice was struck by the **plague** that came from the Orient and, in a short time, exterminated three quarters of the population.

In the years that followed, renewed **rivalry** sprang up **with Genoa** who had taken control of the island of Chios. **The Genoese won in the waters of Bosphorus** in 1353; while the **Venetians were the betters** in the vicinity of Alghero, **in Sardinia**, in 1353, but the **Genoese**, with the help of Giovanni Visconti, lord of Milan, **won again near Methoni** – on the coast of Greece – a year later. For this reason, the **Venetians were obliged to make peace.**

It was a short-lived peace, however, because **Genoa**, with the help of the king of Hungary, **reinitiated hostilities,** and, in 1358, **Venice was obliged to give up** Treviso and many other cities in Dalmatia. In 1379, **war erupted once more** over control of the island of Tenedos, occupied by Venice, but contested by the Genoese. In the same year, **Genoa managed to**

The port of Pisa, in a relief from the 13th century. This seafaring city, together with Genoa, held a blockade against Venetian access.

Chios today. The island was the theater of a battle between Genoa and Venice, which later fought each other during the War of Chioggia.

occupy CHIOGGIA and GRADO, providing an easy communication link with their allies, the Hungarians.

Chioggia was liberated by the Venetians after only one year and, with the help of **Amedeo VI of Savoy**, in 1381, it was stipulated in the **peace of Turin** that Venice had lost its possessions on the mainland but that it would be given total freedom of trade, not only on the sea, but also on land.

In 1402, Venice bought Dalmatia from the king of Hungary, and, in the same year, found itself in **conflict** with PADUA, which, by then, had become a major power because it had absorbed the dukedoms of TREVISO, CONEGLIANO, CENEDA, SERRAVALLE, FELTRE, and BELLUNO, with FRIULI, the big stronghold of the patriarch of AQUILEIA. Venice could not permit the paths of communication between STYRIA, CARINTHIA and AUSTRIA to be controlled by a rival. Therefore, it **allied** itself with **Giangaleazzo Visconti**, Lord of Milan and **Padua**, caught in the crossfire, **was conquered**.

VERONA, VICENZA and PADUA were **annexed to the territories of** MILAN, while Venice was given TREVISO and the communities nearby. **Milan's power,** at this point, seemed to have become excessive and **Venice was prepared to finance the return of the Carraresi family to Padua.** Nevertheless, this friendship with Padua did not last long because **Padua then tried to conquer Verona and Vicenza** which then asked assistance from Venice and agreed to an act of submission.

Such a warlike situation couldn't last long. Venice felt threatened and overall at the mercy of other people's conflicts. It decided to assert itself in order to expand its dominion into the territories directly behind it, and to help any of the cities that had turned to it for help. In 1405, Venetian troops occupied Padua. Padua signed an act of complete surrender to the Republic. Verona, Vicenza, Padua, Rovigo, Treviso, Belluno, Feltre and Ceneda then became territory of the Serenissima. Local ordinances were maintained, but to replace their top officials, members of the Major Council were elected.

In the following years, the expansion of Venice's mainland territories continued. Such a policy forced Venice to be involved in the dramatic events which bloodied the streets of Italy and in which foreign rulers were also involved.

In 1425, Venice allied itself with Florence against Milan; some years later it took possession of Brescia, Bergamo, Crema and Peschiera. In 1433, it intervened in Romania where they were rebelling against the pope, and, in 1441, they forced the Da Polentas who ruled over Ravenna to give up their seignory. In 1448, Venice even tried to overtake Milan, but was forced to draw up a treaty with Francesco Sforza that fixed the borders of the Serenissima to the Adda river. In 1452, another conflict erupted among the Italian states, but a Turkish threat forced Venice to concentrate its energy elsewhere. The **peace of Lodi** in 1454 closed, at least for a certain period, the internal conflicts on the peninsula.

The War of Chioggia, in 1381, established Venice as the master of the Adriatic, in relation to its rival Genoa.

From The Fall Of Constantinople To The Discovery Of America

The fourth crusade, during which Constantinople was sacked and taken over by Venetian forces (1204), put the **crisis of the Eastern Roman Empire** into the spotlight. **The Eastern Latin Empire**, that had then substituted it, was initially entrusted to Baldwin of Flanders and, because of this, all of Venice's commercial privileges were restored. This situation, however, did not last long.

In 1261, **Constantinople** was once again **stormed** by Michael VIII Palaeologus, the Greek that had become its emperor after having managed, with his diplomatic skills, to save the empire from external attacks.

As early as the start of the previous century, a Turkish population coming from the east, and led by Othoman, settled in Asia Minor, substituting itself, little by little with the Selgiuchids who had already been moving in the area for some time. The expansion of the Turkish Ottomans, at the expense of the Byzantine Empire, started early and continued throughout all of the 14th century, until, finally, all of ASIA MINOR was conquered. The Ottomans then overtook the Strait of DARDANELLI and occupied the strip of land between GALLIPOLI and CONSTANTINOPLE launching their attacks in two directions, towards the DANUBE, and towards the territories of the Eastern Empire.

An interesting image of the Grand Canal. In the foreground, Cà Foscari, built in 1452. The façade is an interesting example of a mature Venetian Gothic design.

On the 29th of May, 1452, Mohammed II, after two months of exile, **occupied Constantinople** and slaughtered the inhabitants, among whom were a number of Venetians. Constantine XI died fighting for the ancient Eastern Roman Empire that had, by then, fallen. Constantinople, the ancient Byzatium, once again changed its name; this time to ISTANBUL.

The danger of the Turks forced Venice to abandon its conflicts in the Italian states in order to defend and safeguard its interests in the Orient.

In 1454, **Mohammed II reconfirmed the agreements that Venice had strengthened previously with the Byzantines**, but this situation was not enough to delay the change. The Turks, after having seized the possessions of the Genoese, attacked the Venetians. On the 12th of July, 1470 they occupied the island of NEGROPONT. Then, 1474, they unsuccessfully besieged SCUTARI who fought with heroic resistance. Finally, 1477, a series of raids began in FRIULI which were so bloody that **Venice decided to accept peace** and leave the conquered territories to its enemies (1479).

In the following years, Venice turned its attention once again **to the territories on the mainland** (even if attacks by the Turks continued, interspersed with brief moments of

"Minor" Venice, where feverish preparations for economic activities were made. Together with trade, they made the Serenissima famous.

Above: *The Dogal Palace in a period postcard.* Opposite page: *A detail revealing characteristics of Venetian Gothic.*

peace which, in general, lasted only a short time). In 1503, Venice lost KORONI and METHONI (the two fortresses in Peloponnesus that controlled the Oriental routes), the fortress of LEPANTO (in the Gulf of Corinth) and SANTA MAURA (in the Ionian Sea). Venice could still count on NAUPLION and MONEMVASSIA (on the coast of Peloponnesus), on CEPHALONIA, on ZANTE (for which it had to pay a toll to the Turks) and on its quarter in ISTANBUL, but, in the years to follow, the predominance of the Turks would be more and more insistent.

With the death of **Lorenzo de' Medici**, lord of Florence (1492), the period of relative peace Italy enjoyed after the Peace of Lodi (1454) came to an end. **Ludovico il Moro**, lord of Milan, enlisted the aid of the French king Charles VIII, who, meeting hardly any resistance, descended the peninsula and reached Naples. Only later did Venice, Milan and the pope join forces in a **Holy League** to prevent a foreigner from establishing himself in Italy. The league's armies clashed with the French at FORNOVO (1495), when Charles VIII had already returned to France. ***These events clearly pointed out the political weakness of the Italian states***.

The fall of the Eastern Empire, with the seizing of power by the Turks, not only marked the end of the Byzantines, but also strained **relations between East and West**. The Venetians, who had enjoyed a trade monopoly and sold such goods as silk, ivory and spices on European markets, were now experiencing serious supply difficulties. The Turks, on the other hand, levied outrageous **taxes and tariffs** causing a **rise** in the **prices** of goods which were particularly in demand by transalpine manufacturers. The need to overcome these problems prompted the major European powers to seek new and quicker routes, so as to avoid the Turkish blockade and the monopoly by Venice's merchants.

In 1492, the kingdoms of ARAGON and CASTILLE, united via the marriage of Ferdinand to Isabella, succeeded once and for all in routing the Arabs from the Iberian peninsula. The **Kingdom of Granada**, after a long and bloody siege, **was forced to surrender**. The sovereigns could then turn their attention and resources of the newly formed kingdom to other undertakings. On the 12th of October 1492 **Christopher Columbus**, seeking a new route to the Indies, **landed in America**. With this discovery, the Mediterranean ceased to be the center of the western world.

In 1498, **Vasco de Gama**, a Portuguese navigator, after having doubled the CAPE OF GOOD HOPE sailed to the MALABAR coast, where he loaded up on spices which he brought back to Lisbon without paying a single tariff and without having to cross either deserts or treacherous lands.

Venice's role, as a bridge between East and West, **lost importance**; the Mediterranean was about to become a "small" sea and the Italian peninsula to be utterly overwhelmed by foreigners. The **future of the Serenissima**, at the apex of its splendor, seemed to be in jeopardy.

The Splendor Of The 16th Century

In 1503 Giuliano della Rovere ascended the papal seat as **Julius II**, and was determined to defend the States of the Church against any foreign interference. Even **Venice constituted a threat** to his eyes, both because he feared the presence in Italy of too powerful a state, and also because he wasn't prepared to countenance Venice's conquests in the ROMAGNA region. Then, when the Venetian Republic refused to pay income to Romagna bishops who lacked Venetian citizenship, **Julius II** coalesced all the other Italian states, together with the Empire, France and Spain, in the **League of Cambrai** (December 1508) and launched an attack which was to have utterly annihilated the Serenissima.

On 14th May, 1509, the Venetian army suffered a **bitter defeat** at AGNADELLO which brought about the loss of all the territories Venice had held in LOMBARDY and of most of its hinterland. The end seemed to be in sight. The Florentine historian **Machiavelli**, an enemy of Venice, was convinced

A miniature of the Venetian Arsenal, conserved in the Marciana Library.

that it was; the Italian states, envious of the power Venice had hitherto wielded, were elated; whereas the **king of France** and the **Emperor Maximilian**, who descended to conquer PADUA, hoped this was indeed the case.

Venice, however, **rallied promptly**. All together, both commoners and the nobility, perceiving a common purpose, joined forces and succeeded in defeating Maximilian and in retaking Padua. Diplomatic skills, fine honed by centuries of history, did the rest. Venice stipulated **separate peace treaties** with its adversaries and, on February 24th, 1510, obtained Julius II's "pardon".

The war however did not end and continued even after the pope's death. Venice allied with France and in 1515, after the victorious **battle of Marignano**, regained possession of all its mainland territories.

Late 15th-century Venice in a painting by Vittore Carpaccio. The Rialto bridge was still wooded.

Wars, **sea-trade difficulties**, and the **complex events** of the time ***did not however diminish Venice's splendor***. The city, in fact, was a veritable Renaissance metropolis, with its one hundred and seventy-five thousand inhabitants, and where patricians and the State constantly vied to outdo one another in patronizing the arts.

Rialto and the Grand Canal were embellished by the building of **magnificent new palaces** and of a new bridge, substituting the former draw-bridge. Atop the ***campanile* of San Marco** was hoisted a gold angel; **Titian**, **Tintoretto**, il **Veronese**, together with a host of other artists decorated buildings both sacred and lay; **Palladio** reinterpreted classical antiquity. Cultural life was sparked in every corner of the city. In the CANNAREGIO area **Pietro l'Aretino**'s comedies were performed in a theater with scenes and decorations by **Giorgio Vasari**. Venice was the Mecca of both **French** and **Flemish maestros a cappella**, San Marco's often the stage for grand concerts, whilst the mathematician **Nicola Tartaglia** explained Euclid in the church of Saints John and Paul.

What is more, and despite the Inquisition, ***life in Venice was freer than in any other Italian city.***

The difficult relations with the Turks notwithstanding, **trade with the Orient still proved most profitable**, even though the city's **wealth** was by now also determined by the **various activities** which had developed both in Venice itself and on the mainland. The elegance of **Venetian products**, unequaled in all Europe, helped boost demand for such articles as precious cloths, rare furs, gold-embossed leather, glass, embroidery, lace, ceramics, pewter, copper, jewels and silverware. **On the mainland other kinds of enterprises went up**: weapons industries in BRESCIA where, as early as the late 15th century, there were at least two hundred factories, semi-precious stone concerns in VICENZA and VERONA, carved-wood enterprises in BERGAMO and ISTRIA.

The flurry of myriad new activities, however, was negatively offset by a drop in that of shipbuilding in particular and of maritime activities in general, showing that by now control and development of the mainland had acquired paramount importance for Venetians.

In **1515, the Turks seized hold of Egypt** and two years later defeated the Portuguese who had made inroads in the waters off JEDDA. This victory helped to ensure for the Mediterranean, and therefore especially for Venice, a flour-

A phase of the battle of Lepanto in a period engraving. The Venetians, who had joined the Holy League, destroyed the Turkish fleet, but suffered numerous losses.

ishing and long-lasting spice trade. As the years went by, however, **constant Turkish raids** along the coasts of the Mediterranean became a serious **threat to Christian states**. Furthermore, the Turks had set their sights on the very heart of Europe, to the extent of occupying Budapest in 1541. ***The West simply couldn't just stand by***. In **1569 Cyprus was attacked** by Selim II, successor to Suleiman the Magnificent. NICOSIA, one of the island's most important cities, was finally seized after fifteen attempts. Then it was FAMAGUSTA's turn, the last city which Venice had still managed to control.

Thanks to the **Holy League**, which was signed **on the 20th of May 1571**, Spain, Genoa, the Papal States and Venice joined forces to thwart the infidels. In **August 1571**, the Christian fleet confronted and destroyed the Turks at LEPANTO, in the **biggest and bloodiest naval battle** ever to have been fought in the MEDITERRANEAN, and during which the Venetians bore themselves with heroic distinction.

Despite this significant victory, **Venice**, which had been left to herself by her allies, **failed to regain Cyprus**, and had to make do with the acknowledgment of her trade privileges with the Ottoman Empire. This too sparked the envy and jealousy of the other "allies", who accused the Serenissima of having sold out to the infidel.

Above: *Shrove Tuesday in Venice. Even during war time, the city did not forgo merrymaking.* Below: *The Grand Canal, along whose banks magnificent palaces were built during the 16th century.*

The 17th Century: A Sterile Prosperity

As early as the first decades of the 17th century, **economic activities** in Venice **first experienced troubled times, then a period of considerable stagnation**. Ocean routes to AMERICA and the ORIENT had in fact greatly reduced mercantile traffic on the Mediterranean, which by now was of only secondary importance.

At the **beginning of the century**, Venice still produced approximately thirty thousand pieces of woolen cloths a year, whereas **midway through the century** output failed to exceed ten thousand pieces, and, by the **close of the century**, it had fallen to a mere two thousand. **Competition** from HOLLAND, ENGLAND and FRANCE had become progressively stiffer. In fact, as early as 1599 the English were already trading with the Turks, and starting in 1612 even the Dutch had established similar commercial relationships. Meanwhile, **European interest in spices** in general, and pepper in particular, **had begun to wane**, whereas that in **sugar, tobacco and coffee**, commodities which traveled along ocean routes, **was building**. At the end of the century, the Italian states' fleet accounted for merely seven or eight per cent of the entire European fleet, as compared to ENGLAND's approximately twenty-seven per cent and HOLLAND's seventeen. Throughout the whole century, **Venice was able to maintain her independence** from SPAIN, which had extended its dominion virtually over the entire Italian peninsula, from AUSTRIA, and from the PAPAL STATES. When in **1605** pope **Paul V threatened Venice with interdiction** for having refused to turn over some friars for judgment by ecclesiastical tribunals, the **Republic**, having also been advised by brother **Paolo Sarpi**, a theologian, not to let herself be intimidated, ***reaffirmed its right to conduct its affairs in total autonomy from Rome***. ***Nor was the Republic to be intimidated by Spain***, whose help had been sought by the Papal States. Thus, the pope had to retreat from his position. This is

Portrait of Paolo Sarpi, the theologian who challenged the Inquisition's authority.

why, in the eyes of many men of culture, like Galileo Galilei, ***Venice represented an ideal venue to escape the pressure of the Inquisition***.

The **prosperity of the Venetian republic**, which, although politically isolated, was still a most viable point of reference within Europe's cultural framework, **continued throughout the entire seventeenth century**. In fact, **Venetian merchants utilized the sizeable capital they had previously garnered to purchase farms on the mainland** and reclaim vast swamp-infested areas. They slowly gave up the activities which had absorbed the talents and energies of their forefathers, and took on noble lifestyles, thus living more often than not off their rents.

In order to approach the plague-stricken, physicians covered their faces with a special mask, the inside spout of which contained aromatic spices and herbs to prevent contagion.

The city preserved the **splendor of the preceding century**, and saw the talents of painters, sculptors and especially architects still being put to good use. New churches went up, such as the basilica of **Santa Maria della Salute**, and also magnificent **buildings**, such as the **Pesaro** and **San Stae palaces**, in the halls of which the nobility of the day held its splendid festivities. In **1613 Claudio Monteverdi** was summoned to the city as chapel master at San Marco's.

Besides manifestations of aristocratic splendor, however, displays of ***highhandedness*** by idle noblemen and "bravi", the very same Manzoni so aptly was to describe in his *The Betrothed*, ***were also on the increase***.

The **plague hit Venice in 1630**. In the sole month of August over twenty-four thousand Venetians left the city and moved to the countryside; in the month of November almost fifteen thousand people lost their lives. In November of the following year, when notice had been given to all European courts that the epidemic had abated, Venice counted her dead which numbered over forty-six thousand, more than a quarter of the population.

Meanwhile, ***hard times were in the offing with the Ottoman Empire***, after almost seventy

The Venetian fleet, under the command of Doge Francesco Morosini, takes the fortress of Chios.

years of relative tranquillity ensured by the battle of Lepanto (1571). **Trade with the Orient**, in spite of everything, **continued florid**, even if Venetian repression of the Muslim pirates that infested the MEDITERRANEAN, and especially the ADRIATIC, was not particularly well countenanced by ISTANBUL. In **1638**, off the port of **Valona** the Venetian fleet sunk all of fifteen pirate ships, sparking the ire of the Sultan.

Six years later, in **1644, the Knights of Malta**, a religious-chivalric order founded at the time of the crusades and always ready to fight the "infidels", **attacked a Turkish convoy en route to the Mecca**, which, on the return leg of its journey, in order to seek refuge from a storm, **had docked** along the southern coast of CRETE.

The island had been under Venetian control for four and a half centuries, and the Turks exploited the incident to attempt conquest of a highly strategic area. In the spring of **1645**, four hundred **Ottoman ships** bearing fifty thousand men started a **war** which was to last twenty-four years, and which, despite the heroism of the Venetians led by doge **Francesco Morosini**, ended with the **loss of Crete** (**1669**). Neither did the war spare the Turks, whose power, at the end of the conflict, was greatly diminished. In **1683** their **attempt to occupy** VIENNA **failed**, and in **1684 Venice**, having entered a Holy Alliance with AUSTRIA, RUSSIA and POLAND, occupied MOREA, which was then the name of the PELOPONNESUS, possession of which was subsequently confirmed in the **peace of Karlowitz** on the Drava in **1699**.

This was a vast territory, but unfortunately one which had been impoverished and its population greatly diminished, in which Venice invested heavily. These investments, however, failed to yield the expected fruits, especially as the local inhabitants were ill disposed to accept Venice's organizational structure and mentality. Thus ended a century both complex and splendid, throughout which Venice had experienced considerable economic decadence, but a century during which the city had come through many battles practically unscathed, and without forfeiting either its autonomy or independence.

Venice and the Arsenal in a 17th-century print.

A Splendid Isolation

Starting from the early decades of the 18th century, ***the ideas of Enlightenment figures had begun to spread*** across the various states into which Italy was then divided. Those thinkers, scientists and, more generally, men of culture had entrusted "reason" with the task of not only interpreting reality, but also of modifying it. Venice, still splendid despite its isolation, nevertheless remained extraneous to the reformist movements which were affecting the rest of Europe, especially as the Venetian magistratures had become so rigid as to allow only a few, those particularly well-to-do, the opportunity of taking part in political decision making.

In **1713, with the Treaty of Utrecht**, LOMBARDY gained recognition as a **dominion of Hapsburg Austria**. From **1737**, once the Medici line had become extinct, TUSCANY passed to the **Grand Duke of Lorraine**, the husband of Maria Theresa of Austria. The Dukedom of MODENA, when the Este family became extinct, was given to a **son of Maria Theresa**. In **1769**, with the marriage of Ferdinand, duke of PARMA, to a daughter of Maria Theresa, the duchy fell under **Austrian influence**. In **1778**, even the Kingdom of NAPLES, with the marriage of king Ferdinand IV to another of Maria Theresa's daughters, similarly fell under **Austrian influence**. Spanish dominion of the preceding century was substituted in the 18th century by that of Austria, and once again the **sole Italian state to have preserved its autonomy was Venice**. Feeling itself "besieged", the city did everything in its power to avoid involvement in international political affairs.

A noble Venetian family portrayed by Pietro Longhi.

In **1718**, after almost five years of strife with the Ottoman Empire, **Venice also lost control over the** PELOPONNESUS, the last bulwark of its numerous possessions in the Mediterranean. Thus, what remained to the Republic were DALMATIA, ALBANIA and the IONIAN ISLANDS; on the mainland: TREVISO, BELLUNO and FELTRE, the FRIULI district with ISTRIA, PADUA, ROVIGO, VICENZA, VERONA, the area around SALÒ, BRESCIA, BERGAMO and CREMA.

Hall and stage of Venice's La Fenice Theater, recently destroyed by fire. It was inaugurated in 1792.

The **economic crisis** however was **steadily advancing**, and with it **fiscal pressures increased**, especially at the expense of activities which were linked to the mainland. Landowners resorted ever more frequently to high-yield crops such as grain and vineyards, to the detriment of grazing lands and forests. As a result, the ***ovine population diminished***, thus triggering a wool shortage for the textile industry, as did the ***woodlands***, creating problems for shipbuilding. The ruling class promoted - albeit not always successfully - initiatives aimed at stepping up output, and committed itself to carrying out several public undertakings, the most ambitious of which was without a doubt the **building of the Murazzi**, the huge dam between MALAMOCCO and CHIOGGIA, which was put up to defend the coastline from the ravages of the tidewaters.

In spite of the economic crisis, political isolation and the loss of its island possessions, **18th-century Venice witnessed an extraordinary blooming of the arts**. Giambattista **Tiepolo**, Pietro **Longhi**, **Canaletto**, **Guardi** were the "big names" in painting, around whom gravitated many a master. The **Fine Arts Academy** was rife with talented artists. Antonio **Vivaldi** was for years art director of the **Santa Maria della Pietà Conservatory** in the Riva degli Schiavoni area. Not one evening went by without a concert, sonata or show being performed in one of the city's theaters. Supporters of Carlo **Gozzi**, who in turn supported the traditional *commedia dell'arte*, clashed polemically with those of Carlo **Goldoni**, who approached the theater from a middle-class, realistic perspective, whereas Giacomo **Casanova** portrayed a city obsessed with sex and gambling. Venice's basically lay society was living its last season of independence, in the frenzied midst of sundry revelries, balls and carnivals which elicited the active participation of nobles and plebeians alike.

From Illusion To Betrayal

The Bucintoro, symbol of the Serenissima, pictured here in an 18th-century print. The last such vessel was built in 1727 and almost totally destroyed by order of Napoleon in 1798.

On **July 14, 1789** the people of Paris rose up and stormed the Bastille, the ancient fortress where political prisoners were held. The **French revolution *swept away the privileges of the nobility*** and ***brought to the fore stage*** of political life, in a flurry of dramatic events, ***the bourgeoisie***. The major European powers, which took a dim view of these events, joined forces against France in an attempt to restore the power of the ruling family.

In **1795, the Directory decided to unleash an offensive against Austria** and entrusted **Napoleon Bonaparte** with the task of leading an army which, having first invaded PIEDMONT and LOMBARDY, would attack one of the Austrian fronts.

The almost forty thousand men under Napoleon's command were poorly armed, but the strategic skills of the young Corsican general turned the **Italian campaign** into a veritable triumph.

The Napoleonic venture on the Italian peninsula was initially hailed by some as shackle-breaking. In fact, the ideals put forth by the revolution had sparked the enthusiasm of those who had been nurtured on Enlightenment principles. However, it soon became clear to everyone that the three-colored flag the French troops brought along with them did not herald the changes for which some had hoped.

On **March 20, 1796** Napoleon's campaign got underway. On the **28th of April**, PIEDMONT, defeated, signed the **armistice of Cherasco**, and Vittorio Amedeo III was obliged to cede Savoy and Nice to France. Then, Napoleon moved on to LOMBARDY **clashing head on with the Austrians**, who had previously occupied Venetian holdings on the mainland, despite the Republic's having declared its neutrality. After a hard-won **Napoleonic victory** at LODI, the two armies continued to clash in the area of MANTUA, without either side managing to gain the upper hand. Napoleon then led his armies toward MODENA and REGGIO, where on the **16th of October the Cispadane Republic was founded**, which was the first to hoist the three-colored flag: white, red and green.

A few days later, **Bonaparte resumed hostilities against the Austrians**, and with a series of victories succeeded in occupying almost all the cities in the VENETO-FRIULI area, definitively violating Venetian neutrality in the process. Nevertheless, the French army was in difficulty and Napoleon, sure that he would not be able to reach VIENNA, thought it best to sign an at least temporary peace accord with the enemy. In this connection, ***Venice could prove an excellent bargaining pawn***.

On **May 12, 1797** the **Major Council** was convened for the last time, and with 512 votes in favor, and only 20 against, the decree whereby Venice **abdicated its sovereignty** was passed. Power was transferred to a "**municipality**", selected from among those favoring the French presence. **Venice became a democratic republic**.

On **15 May**, during a popular uprising accompanied by the cry of "Viva San Marco", the Doge abandoned the Dogal Palace and, **for the first time in fifteen centuries, foreign troops entered the city on the lagoon**. Events however precipitated. On **June 26** the **Cisalpine Republic** was proclaimed in MILAN, and on the **29th** the **Austrians**, who had already occupied Dalmatia and Istria, **conquered Zara**.

On the **17th of October 1797**, **Napoleon signed the Treaty of Campoformio**, which ceded all Venetian territories to Austria. On **December 7**, **San Marco's splendid horses** "went off" to PARIS; on the **9th of January 1798**, the Arsenal was destroyed, as was the Bucintoro, symbol of the Serenissima. On **January 18, the French troops left the city** and, on the same day, were **replaced by their Austrian counterparts**.

Signing of the Treaty of Campoformio in a period print.

The Napoleonic Tragedy

On **March 12, 1800**, after a 102-day conclave, Cardinal Gregorio Barnaba Chiaramonti **was elected pope in Venice** in the church of **San Giorgio Maggiorc**, and took the name of **Pius VII**.

Only two years before had Venice become Austrian, the former patricians of the dissolved Major Council having sworn their loyalty to the Austrian emperor on the 22nd of February 1798. Many in Venice, out of resignation, had hailed the dominators as saviors. The **French**, actually, had **despoiled the city of many an art treasure**, and Napoleon's troops had laid waste to the land, committing all sorts of crimes and thefts while they were at it. The Venetian political class no longer had the energy to oppose these events, and no one believed Venice could survive siege by the major powers.

However, in **1805**, with the **Treaty of Presburg**, Napoleon, having become emperor after his defeat of the Austrians, joined the entire VENETO, and therefore also VENICE, ISTRIA and DALMATIA, with the KINGDOM OF ITALY.

Napoleon crosses the Gran San Bernardo, in the celebrated portrayal by David.

On **19 January 1806, French troops again entered Venice** amidst popular enthusiasm (as chronicles of the time reported the event), and **remained there until 1815**. ***There followed ten years of decadence***. Industry was in shambles, as was trade, and shipping had practically come to a halt.

MILAN had become the kingdom's capital, and VENICE fallen to the rank of a **second-rate province**. All the mainland territories formerly belonging to the glorious Serenissima were now assigned to French marshals and generals.

On **November 21, 1806**, in order to overcome the resistance of his fiercest foes, Napoleon decreed a **continental**

blockade on English ships and goods. A decision which was to prove **particularly damaging to Venice**, which was to witness an even further drop in its already dwindling sea trade.

The city's inhabitants suffered a process of impoverishment which was as serious as it was rapid. In a few years' time, one third of the population, almost fifty thousand people, was listed as indigent.

In a satirical print of the time, French "cocks" kill a "lion", symbol of Venice.

The city's art and history heritage suffered as well. Between **1806** and **1810**, numerous religious communities were suppressed, and along with them even seventy-two churches. The church of **San Giminiano**, a Sansovino masterpiece, **was demolished** in order to build in its stead a ball room and a reception hall in the royal palace, which had been installed in the former *Procuratie* in Saint Mark's Square. In order to build a cemetery, the church of **San Cristoforo della Pace** and an **entire city quarter** which housed sacred structures and countless art works, most of which were lost, were razed**. Hundreds of palaces were destroyed**, and with them all their precious contents.

Even though Eugene Beauharnais, who was awarded the title of Prince of Venice in 1807, instituted the galleries of the Fine Arts Academy, and arranged to finance the Marciana Library, Venice lost **more than twenty-five thousand paintings**, among which works by Carpaccio, Tiepolo, Tintoretto, etc.

On **October 21, 1813 the Austrians laid siege** to the city, and on **April 19, 1814**, after the Schiarino Rizzino armistice, they retook possession of a city which was so devastated as to be only a shadow of what it had been up to only a few decades before.

The Risorgimento

On **May 3, 1815**, in the basilica of San Marco, representatives of the Venetian provinces swore **loyalty to Emperor Francis I of Austria**, in the person of his brother, the Archduke **John Baptiste**. On the same day, the **four bronze horses** that the French had stolen eighteen years earlier, were **restored to their former positions**. Recovery of the horses had been brokered by no less a figure than the sculptor **Antonio Canova**.

Thus, the VENETIAN PROVINCES became a part of the **Lombard-Venetian Kingdom**, for which the Austrians established **two capitals**, MILAN and VENICE, both residences of the viceroy, who was chosen from among Austrian dukes. Venice became the **seat of the Royal Navy's high command** and **of the kingdom's Supreme Court of Appeal**.

Between **1813** and **1830**, the **city's population diminished** by approximately twelve thousand people, thus slowly falling to slightly over one hundred thousand inhabitants. The **number of those active** in once florid activities was by now **negligible**, and in 1827 there were only eighty silk looms, whereas the number of wool and linen looms had dropped to only eighteen. Both craft activities in general and sea trade languished. It was only English and French travelers who to some extent buoyed the tourist trade.

Ugo Foscolo: the famous poet, born on the island of Zante, forcefully denounced Napoleon for having betrayed Venice by handing the free Republic over to the Austrians.

Starting in 1838, the situation began to change, after, that is, that important works, like the building of a **railway line linking Milan to Venice** and completion of the Malamocco harbor dam, had been entrusted to private companies. Those years also saw the birth of the **Società Veneta Commerciale**, whose ships not only plied the MEDITERRANEAN but also the ATLANTIC. A river transport system developed along the PO and its tributaries, the **Arsenal provided employment for three thousand workers** who built war ships, and, on **January 15, 1846**, a **railway bridge** over the lagoon was inaugurated.

Venice had not taken part in the 1821/22 Carbonari insurrection, even though the city was not extraneous to reformist ferment. In **1844 Attilio** and **Emilio Bandiera**, who in Venice had founded a secret society by the name of **Esperia**, **died before a firing squad** in COSENZA, after an insurrectional attempt. In those same years, **Daniele Manin**'s ideas enjoyed a rather broad consensus in Venice. If the city was to regain a new identity, he contended that it was necessary to engage in a "legal" confrontation with the Austrian occupiers, around whom a vacuum was to be created. Working in close proximity to him was the Dalmatian **Niccolò Tommaseo**, who, with his passionate oratory succeeded in marshaling the Venetians along a path of freedom and independence.

The Bandiera brothers (above: Emilio, below: *Attilio) executed near Cosenza in 1844, were officers in the Austrian navy. In 1842 joined the Giovine Italia movement.*

On **December 30, 1847**, Niccolò **Tommaseo** held a conference at the Venetian university, "*On the state of Italian letters*", laying claim to **Italian unity** and advocating the abolition of censorship. **Tommaseo** and **Daniele Manin** were **arrested on the 19th of January 1848**. On the 24th of February a **revolution** broke out in PARIS, and on March 17 the news was that in VIENNA too there had been an **uprising** which had forced the powerful minister Metternich to resign. **Manin** and **Tommaseo** were immediately released, and a few days later, on **March 22**, **Venice rebelled and set itself up as the Democratic Venetian Republic presided over by Manin**. Meanwhile, entreated by the Milanese, **Carlo Alberto** had engaged the Austrians, thus prompting Venice to seek annexation to Piedmont. The **first war of independence**, however, failed to unfold favorably, and when Carlo Alberto signed the **Salasco armistice**, **Venice reinstated Manin**, who again assumed control of the government together with Admiral Graziani and Colonel Cavadelis.

Having been definitively **defeated** at NOVARA, on **March 23, 1849 Carlo Alberto** abdicated in favor of his son Victor Emmanuel II. The victorious **Austrians ordered**

Venice to surrender, but the city proclaimed its will to "resist at all costs". Thus, there **began a tragic siege** which lasted up to the month of August. Furthermore, a **cholera** epidemic struck not only the besiegers, but also the mainland inhabitants, who had already been sapped by famine. Mortality soared. More than four hundred people died daily either of disease, privation or struck down by enemy artillery fire. The city was devastated by fires, craft shops closed. On July 29 intense shelling began, and twenty days later, on August 22, 1849, **Venice had to capitulate**.

Manin and forty other patriots were exiled. Venice, prostrated by the siege, famine and cholera, had to undergo further impoverishment which, at least in part, undermined the economic recovery of the thirties and forties. ***Venice's history, starting in August 1849, followed the events of the burgeoning unitary state***.

In **1859**, **Cavour**'s political plan led to Napoleon III's France forming an alliance with Piedmont against Austria. It seemed that the moment for Venice to rid herself of Austrian dominion had arrived. However, when the French emperor, at the end of the **second war of independence**, together with Franz Josef signed the **armistice of Villafranca** granting PIEDMONT only the region of LOMBARDY, another **difficult period** was in the offing for the water-girded city. Four-thousand five-hundred people, among whom entrepreneurs, intellectuals, men of talent and culture, opted for exile, thus further depleting the city of the necessary energies for survival.

Daniele Manin in a caricature of the time.

In **1866**, five years after the Italian kingdom had been proclaimed, an Italo-Prussian alliance set the stage for the **third war of anti-Austrian independence**. On October 19, Italian troops entered the city which, as the result of a **plebiscite**, became Italian two days later. ***The Risorgimento had come full circle***.

During the **final decades of the century**, Venice witnessed a significant economic, political and cultural **recovery**, as can be evinced by the quality of the many newspapers which were printed there, and by the **urban improvement initiatives**, which nevertheless sparked no mean amount of controversy. The first **Biennial International Exhibition of Contemporary Art** was inaugurated on **April 22, 1895**. In 1902, San Marco's belfry collapsed, but was immediately rebuilt. In 1917, during the First World War, an agreement to construct an **industrial area** near MARGHERA met with approval; in 1933 a road bridge crossing the lagoon was inaugurated; in 1938 a law guaranteeing preservation of the city's lagoon character was passed, etc. At this point, history becomes the chronicling of everyday events.

The arrival of Neapolitan troops in Venice in 1848. The city on the lagoon enjoyed the solidarity of other Italian cities, but nevertheless failed to hold out against the Austrians.

Basic Chronology

302 BC	Cleomenes of Sparta's expedition in the Venetian lagoon
421 AD	Legendary founding of Venice
476	Fall of the Western Roman Empire
493	Theodoric, king of the Ostrogoths, establishes himself in Ravenna
526	Death of Theodoric
527	Justinian is crowned Roman Emperor of the East
540	The Byzantine General Belisarius conquers Ravenna
562	The Longobards descend upon Italy
556	Death of Justinian
568	The Longobards occupy Friuli
602	The Longobards burn Padua and destroy Altino
638/639	Founding of Cittanova (*Eraclea*) in the lagoon
640	First stone laid of the Torcello cathedral
680	Truce between Byzantines and Longobards
697	Election of the first doge Paulicio, according to Giovanni Diacono's chronicle
713/715	Election of the first doge Paulicio, according to the *Cronicon Altinatae*
751	Ravenna is conquered by the Longobards
756	Astolfus, king of the Longobards, cedes to Pippin, king of the Franks, the Exarchate of Ravenna
774	Charles, king of the Franks, brings about the fall of the Longobard dynasty
800	Charlemagne is crowned Emperor of the Holy Roman Empire
810	Peace treaty between Byzantines and Charlemagne: Venice is given to Byzantium
828	Venetians welcome the remains of Saint Mark the Evangelist, purloined in Alexandria
883	Venice attacks and devastates Comacchio

992	Otto III, Emperor of the West, confirms the privileges of Venice
1071	End of Byzantine domination in southern Italy
1082	Venice receives from Byzantium complete tax exemption to promote the trading activities of Venetian merchants
1098	Pope Urban III institutes the first Crusade to liberate the Holy Land
1099	Pisans and Venetians clash on Rhodes
1104	Venetian victories at Jaffa and Sidon
1142/1144	The Emperor of Byzantium stipulates an agreement with the Genoese
1143	Institution of the Council of the Wise
1152	Frederick Barbarossa ascends the throne of the Holy Roman German Empire
1167	Venice adheres to the Lombard League, as does the pope
1172	The Council of the Wise takes one the name of Grand Council and is flanked by a Lesser Council
1177	Peace between Frederick Barbarossa and Pope Alexander III in San Marco's
1201	Venice promotes the fourth Crusade
1203	The Venetians occupy Byzantium
1204	Baldwin of Flanders is elected Latin Emperor of the East
1207	The Venetians occupy Corfu
1207/1212	The "Quarantia" is born
1209/1210	The Venetians conquers Crete
1218	Treaty with Genoa
1253	Treaty with Genoa broken
1255	The Council of the Rogati is founded
1271	Marco Polo leaves for China
1284	Minting of the gold ducat
1297	Lockout by the Major Council

1298	The Genoese defeat the Venetians at Curzola
1302	Trade agreement with Egypt
1310	The Council of the Ten is instituted
1333	Trade agreement with the Tartars
1337	Mastino II della Scala cedes Treviso, Ceneda and Castelfranco to Venice
1348	The black plague rages throughout Europe and also in Venice
1373	The Genoese occupy Famagusta
1378	The Genoese are defeated at Anzio
1379/1380	A general estimate is compiled
1380	The Genoese are defeated at Chioggia
1404	Vicenza, Feltre and Belluno are ceded to Venice
1405	Verona is ceded, and Padua defeated
1425	Venice and Florence ally against Milan
1426	Brescia is conquered
1433	Venice intervenes in Romagna
1448	Navigation eastward is suspended
1448	Treaty with Milan to establish the borders of the Serenissima
1452	After a two-month siege, Mohammed II occupies Constantinople and massacres Venetians
1454	Peace of Lodi
1470	The Turks occupy the Island of Negropont (*Euboea*)
1474	Siege of Scutari
1477	Raids of the Turks in Friuli
1479	Venice gives up its territories by the sea occupied by the Turks
1495	Battle of Fornovo
1503	Venice loses Koroni and Methoni
1508	League of Cambrai
1509	Battle of Agnadello
1515	Battle of Marignano
1569	Selim II attacks Cyprus
1571	The Christian fleet of the Holy League confronts and destroys the Turkish fleet at Lepanto

1605	Pope Paul V threatens Venice with interdiction
1630	The plague hits Venice
1644	The Turks attempt to conquer Crete
1645	Doge Francesco Morosini leads the Venetians against the Turks
1669	Venice loses Crete
1684	Venice occupies the Peloponnesus
1699	Peace of Karlowitz
1718	Venice loses control of the Peloponnesus
1796	Italian campaign of Napoleon Bonaparte against the Austrians
1797	Treaty of Campoformio: Napoleon cedes Venice to Austria
1814	Venice becomes a part of the Lombard-Venetian Kingdom
1848/1849	The Venetian Republic of Daniele Manin has to capitulate to Austria
1866	Venice becomes a part of the Kingdom of Italy

Urban Development

Venice's **historic nucleus** rose in the **rivus altus** area, today commonly known as the Grand Canal, and around **Saint Mark's Square**. The **dwellings**, built on piles, **were initially wooden** and surrounded the **first churches** to be erected on the small archipelago of islands dotting the canal. The seat of the magistrature was the **Dogal Palace**, next to which rose the **Convent of San Zaccaria** with its large garden. Beside this cultivated plot, known as the *brolo,* in the IX century the **basilica** which was to house the mortal remains of **Mark** the Evangelist was erected. Between the 11th and the 14th centuries Venice was protected from the sea by **fortifications** which, starting from the OLIVOLO island (later called Castello) continued along the RIVA DEGLI SCHIAVONI up to the GRAND CANAL, which was closed off with heavy chains. Later, these fortifications were eliminated and the city developed with the building of large structures. **Saint Mark's Square**, with its adjoining *piazzetta*, the Dogal Palace and the basilica, was **the city's political and representational center**, while the **Grand Canal** was its **commercial hub**, with its docks for the unloading of goods. Up to the end of the 15th century, the Rialto bridge, then wooded, was centrally mobile, thus allowing boats to pass. Around these two important hubs, besides the **more ancient churches** (the 5th-century San Giacomo and the 7th-century San Salvatore churches), today are still to be found the remains of buildings erected between the 12th and the 13th centuries, such as the **Farsetti** and **Loredan palaces**. On the other hand, in the course of successive centuries the more sumptuous palaces of the nobility went up along the Grand Canal. The **residential districts** rose in the more **off-centered areas**, which often also housed **monasteries**.

The Rialto Bridge, wooden up to the end of the 15th century (below, in a painting by Vittore Carpaccio), was substituted by the structure that can presently be admired.

In the 16th century, the city's historic center reached its maximum expansion. The **Arsenal**, which was already operative in the 13th century in the city's eastern area, was broadened to the extent of becoming the largest shipyard in the entire Mediterranean. **New fortifications** were put up to defend the harbor, as well as new buildings around Saint Mark's Square. **Sansovino** initiated a veritable **Renaissance-style urban reform**, systematically enclosing the city's major buildings (the **Zecca**, the **Marciana Library**, the **Procuratie**, the **Loggetta of the campanile**, in a given area. **Palazzo Ducale** was completed both inside and out. The ancient wooden **Rialto bridge** was replaced by a **stone structure**. The **Fabbriche Nuove** of Rialto, the convents of **San Giorgio**, **San Francesco della Vigna** and **San Salvatore** were all erected in that period. At the end of the century, the new foundations (*Fondamenta nuove*) were built along the city's northern border.

Venice's historic urban core has preserved to this day, even in the most working-class neighborhoods, the "flavor" and charm of the past.

The following two centuries were characterized by the **Baroque**. Thus, there rose such palaces and monumental works as the **Basilica della Salute**. Streets were paved, theaters like **La Fenice** were constructed, building of the **Murazzi** (seawall) got underway in order to defend the city from the fury of the Adriatic.

The fall of the Venetian Republic, with the Treaty of Campoformio, also marked the beginning of **urban decadence**. Structures were **demolished** and spaces widened to make room for the **Royal Gardens**; the Procuratie Nuove were turned into the Royal residence; a canal was covered over in the Castello area and the Riva degli Schiavoni was widened.

During the 19th century, Venice was subsequently connected to the mainland via a **railway bridge** (1846); the **two steel bridges of the Railway** and **the Accademia** went up over the Grand Canal; and the picturesque Santa Marta embankment gave way to the **Stazione Marittima**.

The setting-up of a **seaside resort on the Lido**, the **industrial port** at MARGHERA, **Piazzale Roma**, the **Tronchetto**, etc., are instead 20th-century modifications which, in the opinion of some, have failed to enhance the Serenissima's charm.

Saint Mark's Square And Environs

The Tetrarchs, folded in a symbolic embrace, defend the Dogal Palace from the high water.

Rectangular, closed off on its northern boundary by the **Torre dell'Orologio** built in 1496 and by the **Procuratie Vecchie** – the ancient seat of the Magistrates of San Marco's – delimited westward by the **Napoleonic Wing** and southward by the **Procuratie Nuove** built between the 16th and the 17th centuries, Saint Mark's Square is characterized eastwardly, where it opens onto the lagoon, by the **Basilica** erected to house the mortal remains of **Mark** the Evangelist, which, according to legend, had been purloined by two merchants in EGYPT. Standing by itself, on the opposite side of the square, there rises over 90 meters tall the **campanile**, at the base of which lies **Sansovino**'s marble **loggetta**.

This is the very core of the city, the part which witnessed the Republic's thousand-year history and its many and sundry vicissitudes.

In Byzantine Romanesque style, with its five oriental-style domes, **the Basilica of San Marco**, built as a chapel of the doges on the example of the church of the Twelve Apostles in Constantinople, offers the onlooker a two-tiered façade. The terrace dividing the two levels houses the **gilded horses** dating back to the 3rd century BC. In the atrium, whose vaults are covered with 13th-century mosaics, are the three portals. The church, shaped in the form of the **Greek cross** and divided in one nave and two aisles per each wing, with dividing columns supporting the women's gallery, emits a golden light which is caught and reflected by the **mosaics** gracing both the walls and the vaults. Originally, the work of Venetian-Byzantine masters, the mosaics, partly redone following designs by Titian, Tintoretto and Veronese, portray Christ, the Virgin Mary, the Prophets, the Apostles and, in the central dome, the Ascension. Hidden by the ciborium on the altar is the **Pala d'oro** (the gold altar-piece), a

10th-century Byzantine masterpiece of the goldsmith's craft.

Palazzo Ducale, residence of the doges, faces instead **the *piazzetta* of San Marco's**, and little is known of its original aspect. Starting from the second half of the 14th century, however, its **monumental architecture** took shape, and continued to evolve into elegant Gothic-Venetian forms, with its **Sala del Maggior Consiglio** and a vast array of sculptures and paintings. Those same decades witnessed work on the exterior decorations, which bear the influence of Lombard and Tuscan artistry. **Antonio Rizzo**, a major exponent of Venetian art, was the author of the Scala (staircase), subsequently called the Giants' staircase, with its statuary by Sansovino, and of the courtyard's inner façade. The Palazzo, a veritable **maze of rooms** having an incredible variety of dimensions, suffices to exemplify the intense richness of life during the Venetian Republic.

Facing the Dogal Palace, on the western side of the *piazzetta*, is the **Libreria Vecchia**, in pure Venetian style, similarly designed by Sansovino, which is the original seat of the **Marciana Library** which houses a trove of illuminated manuscripts, together with works by Titian, Tintoretto and Veronese.

Piazzetta *San Marco with the Dogal Palace and the Marciana Library.*

The Grand Canal

The **Grand Canal**, the busy waterway that crosses Venice's historic core, is a veritable open-air museum along which, over the centuries, the nobility of the Serenissima vied to leave the **mark of their own magnificence**. Yet, the Grand Canal, the *rivus altus*, was originally an estuary port where seafaring vessels could dock. Along the canal, there was only one bridge that linked the two main hubs of city life – the politico-representational of **Saint Mark's Square** and the commercial-mercantile of the wharves and market places – vestiges of which still remain in the bridge area which took its name from that of the original waterway (**Rialto**).

Journeying along the waters of the Grand Canal enables the visitor to discover jewels of incalculable value, some of which still await to be rescued from conditions of neglect and the ravages of time. Our itinerary begins before reaching the **Ponte degli Scalzi**, facing the railway station, where there stands the 17th-century church of **Sant'Andrea della Zirada**, now desecrated, which is famous for its **Tintorettos**. Opposite, there is to be admired the 18th-century green dome of **San Simeone and Guido**, which so sparked Napoleon's curiosity.

Beyond the bridge, just before reaching the Cannaregio Canal, stands the church of **San Geremia**, opposite the **Fondaco dei Turchi** (the Turks' Warehouse), now completely restored and seat of the **National History Museum**, which bears lasting witness to the intense trade relations with the ORIENT. Slightly further on, on the opposite bank of the canal, there stand out, among aristocratic palaces, **Palazzo Vendramin**, residence of one of

the most ancient Venetian families, where Richard Wagner lived and died, and the **Ca' d'Oro**, built in 1422, the façade of which, now covered in polychrome marble, was once gilded. Today it is a gallery where visitors can admire, among others, works by **Mantegna**, **Guardi** and **Pontorno**. Centrally located, but on the other side of the **Ca' Pesaro** canal, is the baroque structure by **Longhena**, today the seat of the **Gallery of Modern Art** and of the **Oriental Art Museum**. Immediately after the **Pescheria** there rises the **Rialto bridge**, a one-span stone structure crossed by three flights of stairs onto which open artisan workshops, just as they once did. Near the bridge, the 18th-century church of **San Bartolomeo**, bears past witness to a rather considerable German community residing in Venice. Slightly further on, but more inwardly situated, the 16th-century church of **San Salvatore** conserves a celebrated altar-piece of the Annunciation painted by **Titian** in 1566.

Above and on opposite page: *various views of the Grand Canal, the* Rivus Altus *along which the history of the Serenissima unfolded.*

Moving along towards San Marco's basin, palaces and churches appear to become even more opulent. The right bank is lined with such palaces as the **Ca' Pisani**, **Ca' Balbi**, the Renaissance-style **Ca' Foscari**, the baroque-style **Ca' Rezzonico** and, near the bridge, the **Accademia**, connected to the church of **Santa Maria della Carità** via **Palladio**'s stairway. Along the opposite bank, there stands out, among other noteworthy structures, **Ca' Mocenigo**.

Beyond the **Accademia bridge**, the Grand Canal broadens on one side with the baroque church of **Santa Maria della Salute**, by **Longhena**, which contains paintings by **Titian** and **Tintoretto**, and on the other side with **Ca' Giustinian**.

Island And Islets

From the outset, Venice's history unfolded throughout the entire lagoon, on its numerous islands, both large and small, which emerged protected by the shoreline; but, with the passing of time, centered around those surrounding the **Grand Canal**. For the other islands, history was to have other events in store. Many, in fact, simply disappeared (of the almost one hundred and fifty islands described by an 18th-century cartographer, only about thirty have survived), others merely preserve the vestiges of a glorious past, while others continue to be lively and are at least as famous throughout the world as Saint Mark's Square or the Dogal Palace. Their buildings, whether sacred or lay, and the sundry activities which unfolded on them, are in themselves pages wherein we can read ***an important chapter in the history of the Serenissima***.

The excellent trade links between Venice and the Orient enabled the city on the lagoon to develop from the 10th to the 11th centuries all the activities connected with the **manufacture of glass** and **glassware**. Because of safety reasons, these activities were transferred to MURANO, which, although sufficiently isolated from the city center, was nevertheless quite easy to reach. This way, the city was able to avoid the risk of fires and toxic gas fumes involved in glass manufacturing, while at the same time controlling a highly significant economic activity. Initially, what were produced were especially **common, every-day objects**, such as oil or wine bottles, cups and plates. Soon after, however, in their laboratories craftsmen started turning out **colored and gilded stained glass windows for churches** or **glass for mosaics**. The skill of Murano's master glassmakers soon earned these artisans world fame and, for a few centuries, ***they were***

Glass manufacturing in a Murano craftsman's workshop.

able to vie successfully with the fiercest European competition, particularly that coming from Bohemian glassworks. Only at the end of the 18th century and the beginning of the 19th was the island's glass-manufacturing activity hit by a serious **crisis**, brought about on one hand by the **industrial output** of GERMANY, GREAT BRITAIN, HOLLAND and FRANCE, and, on the other, by the Venetian Republic's **loss of autonomy** with the Treaty of Campoformio. During the second half of the 19th century, however, ***Murano's glass industry again became buoyant***, thus enabling the entire island to preserve a centuries-old tradition.

Above and below: *the colors of Burano's houses have by now become well-known worldwide.*

Boreana was the name of one of the gates of ALTINO, the mainland town whose inhabitants fled to the islands of the Venetian lagoon for fear of barbarian invaders. Almost certainly the name of BURANO, the island known worldwide for its **lace** and for the **color varieties** of its dwellings, ranging from soft to gaudy, derives from that ancient gate. Originally, the settlement was administratively subordinate to TORCELLO, but in the 13th century numerous religious communities gave rise to convents and churches, which today have almost completely disappeared. The parish church of **San Martino**, instead, dates to the 16th century, whereas its characteristic leaning belfry was built in the early 18th century. In the 19th century Burano became ***an important center throughout the entire northern area of the lagoon***.

Lying in a northeasterly direction, and inhabited from the very first decades of the 5th century, TORCELLO was without doubt Venice's progenitor. Located a dozen kilometers from the town's present nucleus, its original name was *Nuova Altino*. Its present name, like that of Burano's, seems to have originated from that of a gate in ancient Altino, subsequently abandoned for fear of the Huns and Longobards. In the 7th century, it became the seat of Paul's bishopric, and the Byzantine empire directly exercised its authority over the area through its *magister militum*. Construction of the cathedral

Above: *walking toward the center of Torcello, to get "involved" in the "sacred quality" of its churches.* Opposite page: *detail of the mosaics in the Santa Maria Assunta cathedral.*

dedicated to the Virgin Mary (**Santa Maria Assunta**), in the foundations of which was found a tablet recording the election of Venice's first doge, dates back to 639. When the Venetian magistrature and Venice's principal activities were transferred to RIALTO, that is along the Grand Canal, ***Torcello slowly began its decline***, a victim also of malaria. Today, the island still has its 7th-century cathedral, which was rebuilt in the 11th century, and **Santa Fosca**, an octagonal Romanesque church, belted on five sides by a portico and with a Greek-cross interior plan, to remind us of its intense religious history.

Besides the major islands, which are also prime tourist attractions, even the smaller islands tell us of Venice's past, scattered as they are here and there between the two large basins dividing the lagoon from the city historic center.

In the same basin where there emerge the major islands, visitors can admire **San Francesco del Deserto**, which owes its name to the Saint of Assisi. In 1220, in fact, Francis visited the island, and after a few years a minor Franciscan order founded a monastery which was to be abandoned two centuries later. The Franciscans returned there in 1858, when the Austrians consigned the monastery to the patriarch of Venice. **The Lazzaretto Nuovo island**, at the mouth of the Sant'Erasmo canal, initially afforded hospitality only to hermits. At the end of the 15th century, it became a depository for whatever goods were suspected of spreading contagious diseases, and in the 18th century it housed the plague-stricken.

Poveglia, the former *Popilia*, rises instead in the southern basin, almost opposite MALAMOCCO, the ancient seat of the city's first nucleus. Its name derives from one of the Roman roads which crossed the lagoon and which was a **thriving and autonomous hub** up to the end of the 14th century. It then became the seat of **naval shipyards**, a **lazaretto** for the plague-stricken, a **shelter** for the quarantined, etc.

Continuing along the lagoon toward Lido, one reaches the **Lazzaretto Vecchio**, the ancient hospice for the plague-stricken which was subsequently used as a military depository and, in more recent times, as a refuge for stray dogs. Slightly further on, one meets **San Lazzaro degli Armeni** which, formerly a leper house since 1182, in the 18th century became an important **Armenian culture center**, well-known for its monastery, library and printing-house, which has such a rich number of type characters as to be able to print books in almost forty languages.

At **San Servolo**, located between San Lazzaro and San Gregorio Maggiore, the Benedictines founded one of their monasteries in the 7th century, and remained there for five centuries before surrendering the structure to nuns. Between 1734 and 1759 a psychiatric hospital was built on the site.

The island of **Santa Maria della Grazia**, also called Santa Maria della Cavana, more commonly known as La Grazia, was consolidated thanks to the Venetians' habit of using the island as a dump for their city's refuse. In 1264 a building was constructed to house pilgrims on their way to the Holy Land. Later, the island became a **powder magazine**, and subsequently the site of a hospital.

The Doge, A Symbol Of The Serenissima

Doge Leonardo Loredan, with his elegant headpiece, in a painting by Giovanni Bellini; property of a London museum.

For over a thousand years Venice's supreme magistrate was the doge, and legend, more than history, has handed down to us the name of the first man to assume this title: **Paulicio Anafesto**, elected according to the chronicler **Giovanni Diacono** in 697 or, according to the *Cronicon Altinate*, between 713 and 715. According to others, however, the first doge was **Orso Ipato**, elected in 727, after a military revolt which ended tragically with the killing of Ravenna's exarch. Venice, in fact, at the time was subordinate to the Byzantine Empire which had extended its dominion to the Italian peninsula, and had yet to attain full autonomy. As time passed, however, Venice managed to achieve independence and the doge, who under Byzantine rule flanked the *magister militum* in matters of civil administration, acquired increasing importance.

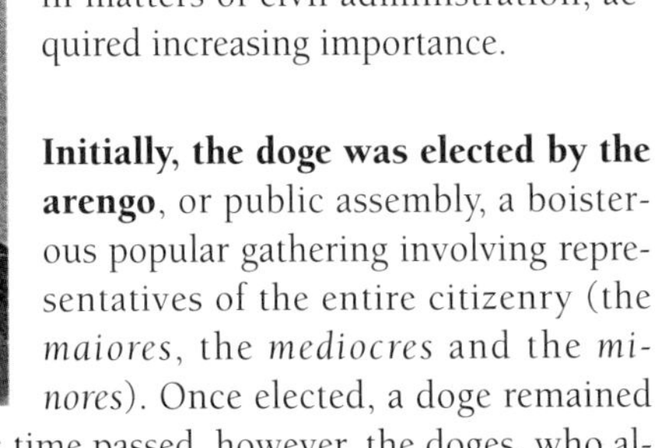

Initially, the doge was elected by the arengo, or public assembly, a boisterous popular gathering involving representatives of the entire citizenry (the *maiores*, the *mediocres* and the *minores*). Once elected, a doge remained in office for life. As time passed, however, the doges, who always came from the most important families, tried in every way possible (and at times successfully) to ensure dogeship for their descendants.

In reality, the doge's authority had always to measure itself with that of the Venetian aristocracy and, as time elapsed, had to undergo numerous limitations. As early as the 9th century, when it was necessary to take important foreign policy decisions, the doge would convene and sound the assembly. Starting from the 12th century, at the moment of his election, the doge had to sign a document, called *promissione*, whereby he pledged to abide by an ever-increasing list of restrictions.

The year 1172 witnessed the birth of the **Consiglio Maggiore** and the **Consiglio Minore**, made up by the *sapientes*, who oversaw every activity of the doge, even the most banal. From 1207 the Consiglio Maggiore was empowered to decide on all state appointments. As the Consiglio Maggiore comprised numerous members, it was deemed expedient to institute less numerous bodies, but with more clearly defined powers: the **Quarantia**, which mainly addressed judicial matters, and the **Senato**, which focused on political issues. In 1310 the **Council of the Ten**, initially set up, as was customary, to investigate one of the many conspiracies that inflamed the Republic's political scene, became a permanent institution, having various attributions, usually of a juridical nature.

In this portrait of Sebastiano Venier, whose dogeship coincided with the second half of the 16th century, it can be seen how the ermine collar, which initially was rather plain, had evolved.

In 1297, Venice passed a law **ensuring that those who had participated for at least four years in the Major Council** were entitled to be **life-long members**; a right which was also guaranteed to their offspring. The **Serrata del Maggior Consiglio**, as was called the law limiting participation in the city's most important body to few families, was perfected thanks to a successive series of other laws which progressively reduced the doge's scope of action.

In 1275 the doge was **forbidden to establish family bonds with foreign princes**; in 1339 he was **forbidden to abdicate**; in 1343 the **doge's sons were denied the possibility of covering whatever public office**; from 1367 **no doge could enjoy the privilege of owning land outside the republic**, and so on.

To celebrate Doge Alvise Pisani's election, a sumptuous villa was built at Strà sul Brenta.

In short, from the 14th century the **Gran Consiglio**, and especially the **Senato**, became the ***state's core institutions***. Their members met daily and were presided over by the doge. The Signoria, also called Serenissima, **the Republic's executive body**, consisted of the **doge**, **six sapientes**, the doge's councilmen, and **three Quarantia notables**. This way, neither one man nor one family could have control of the city.

The progressive reduction in power however was offset by a progressive **increase in the magnificence** with which the doge appeared before the Council, foreign kings and princes, and in all public occasions before the citizenry. In the beginning, his appellative was *messer lo doxe*, but, starting from the 12th century, his title was that of **Serenissimo**.

He would appear aboard the **Bucintoro**, his special vessel which became the symbol of the Republic. His clothes became increasingly more sumptuous, and he wrapped himself in a **scarlet-red mantle**, which, initially short and later long and full-flowing, was fastened by a gem-studded clasp and topped off by an **ermine collar**. Headgear was always given particular importance. In the early days of the Republic, doges wore a rather simply **Byzantine cap** called *zoia*. Eventually, however, and in compliance with guidelines set down by the magistrates, this headgear became more and more elaborate. It was made of damascened or gold-threaded cloth, and at times of crimson velvet, and was decorated with such precious stones that, after each solemn ceremony, it was safely stored away with the State treasury. Under such an imposing headpiece the doge sported a **sheer-linen bonnetlike headdress** fastened below his chin.

Even though the laws increasingly limited the doge's effective authority, no one could claim that their function was purely representational. In fact, many of them bravely played **leading roles in praise-worthy undertakings**, others displayed **great diplomatic skills**, whereas there also were those who brought upon themselves the scorn of the Venetians and were put to death for their crimes or for their attempts to seize power.

In this connection, it is enough to recall **Pietro Orseolo II**, who around the year 1000 had extended the Venetian borders in ISTRIA and DALMATIA, or the representatives of the **Dandolo** family. **Enrico**, elected doge in 1192, contributed significantly to the positive outcome of the **fourth crusade**, during which even CONSTANTINOPLE was conquered. **Andrea** died fighting the Genoese during the **battle of Curzola** in 1298. **Francesco** defeated the Scaligeri of Verona thus paving the way for **Venice's development on the mainland**. Even **Andrea Contarini**, a late 14th-century doge, prove inspirational in promoting Venetian resistance to Genoa at the time of the **War of Chioggia** (1379-80). Lastly, **Alvise Mocenigo**, a wise **diplomat**, had the honor of welcoming to Venice Henry III of France and Francesco Morosini, known as the Peloponnesiac for having conquered Morea.

Among those who, on the other hand, prompted harsh reactions, it is worth remembering **Marino Falier**, doge from 1354, who was defeated by the Genoese and, accused of wanting to set up a dictatorship in Venice, was **condemned** and **decapitated only one year after being elected**.

The "mouth" whereby to report those guilty of undermining public health. Denunciations, even if from anonymous sources, were one of the ways the Council of the Ten controlled city life.

The Art World

Volumes would be needed to do justice to the world of art which developed in Venice over the centuries. However, here we cannot help but mention the extraordinary genius of some of those painters, sculptors and architects who contributed so significantly to Venice's becoming a point of reference not only for all Europe, but for the Orient as well.

If the work of architects and sculptors is readily recognizable from palace façades and in the elegant forms of arcades, bell-towers and cathedrals, the painters' genius comes through in the vault frescoes of buildings both sacred and lay, in the rooms of the most stately homes, in the countless art galleries and museums which are all well worth a visit.

Initially, Venice experienced the ***influence of Byzantine culture***, which was to prove a determining factor for the architecture of the first churches, even for those built, or rebuilt, around the 11th century. In fact, the **Basilica of San Marco** itself duplicates the forms of the Twelve Apostles' church in Constantinople, while Byzantine-style mosaics are to be found even in the most ancient churches, such as the **Torcel-**

Venice's art heritage was sacked by Napoleon's troops, after the Treaty of Campoformio. The print shows the removal of San Marco's bronze horses, which were returned to the city eighteen years later.

lo cathedral, dedicated to Our Lady of the Assumption. It is only from the 13th century that Byzantine influence starts giving way to a more typically Venetian style, the "**flowery Gothic**", which was to account for the city's unique look, and which was applied – especially in civil architecture – up to the end of the 15th century. Emblematic of this style is the **Ca' d'Oro**, the palace that **Bartolomeo Buon**, a Venetian, and **Matteo Raverti**, a Lombard, built for the Contarini family. The **Gothic style**, however, took on more austere forms in the larger churches, such as the **Basilica dei Frari** and that dedicated to **Saints John and Paul**, which are characterized by brick structures and apsidal fretted-marble decorations.

View of the Ca' d'Oro courtyard, an example of Venetian Gothic.

Fifteenth-century Venetian painting, on the other hand, was influenced by **Andrea Mantegna** (1431-1506), who was active in Padua almost in the same years as Donatello, and especially in Mantua, effecting an admirable synthesis between Tuscan styles and Venetian color patterns. **Giambellino** (1432-1516), **Mantegna**'s brother-in-law and pupil, was the master under whose influence Venetian painters gave their best. Together with Giambellino, **Vittore Carpaccio** (famous for his serial paintings for the Sant'Orsola school, now preserved in the Accademia Galleries), aptly captured the customs of his time on his canvases.

Between the late 15th and the 16th centuries, the major painters of the time were active in Venice. In fact, it was in this period that **Giorgio da Castelfranco**, called **Giorgione** (1478-1510), worked in the Serenissima, and paved the way for **Tiziano Vecellio** (1488-1576), practically his contemporary, and for **Tintoretto** (1518-1594).

What remains in Venice today of Giorgione, a master in the use of colors, is ***The Tempest*** and a few fresco traces in the

Pietro Longhi depicted scenes of everyday life. This painting (property of Ca' Rezzonico) represents the polenta *ritual.*

Fondaco dei Turchi. Titian, on the other hand, who was present at all the Renaissance courts of his day, left many more works of art, such as the **frescoes in the Basilica dei Frari**, which he painted in his youth upon arriving in Venice from his native Cadore, and the ***Martyrdom of Saint Lawrence*** in the church of the Jesuits.

Jacopo Robusti, known as **Tintoretto**, was long active in his city, where he worked for the wealthy aristocratic families and for the state, both of which vied to manifest their interest in art patronage. Examples of his most well-known achievements are his decorations of the **Dogal Palace**, the **Schools** of **Saint Mark** and **Saint Rocco**, the church of **San Giorgio Maggiore** and that of the **Madonna dell'Orto**.

Paolo Caliari, called **Veronese**, instead was active in the second half of the century, painting mythological themes both in public buildings, as the Dogal Palace, and in the villas which the aristocracy of the day had built in the country, such as the **Villa Barbaro** at MASER.

It was the century in which **Palladio** designed **San Giorgio Maggiore** and the **church of the Redeemer** in Venice, and left in his splendid Venetian villas the hallmark of a harmonious and finely detailed architecture. Side by side with his sober architectural achievements, those very years also witnessed the construction of buildings by another leading artist. After having worked at the Roman court, **Jacopo Sansovino** spend an extended period in Venice, where, among other works, he designed the **Marciana Library**, the **Zecca** (the Mint), the **Loggetta** of San Marco's belfry, and the **Palazzo Corner**.

If the 17th century saw the aristocratic genius of **Baldassare Longhena**, that master of baroque architecture who designed such grand works of art as the **Scalone** (staircase) **of San Giorgio**, the **Pesaro** and **Rezzonico Palaces**, and the cathedral of **Santa Maria della Salute**, which was consecrated in 1630, the 18th century was the time of great painters like **Tiepolo**, the **Guardi** brothers – Gian Antonio and Francesco – **Canaletto** and **Pietro Longhi**.

Keeping his distance from baroque monumentalism, **Giambattista Tiepolo** succeeded in scenographically interpreting the **myths** and **allegories** of Venetian culture, and frescoed palaces, villas and churches both in Venice and other countries. **Gian Antonio Guardi** specialized in **character portraits**, as did **Pietro Longhi**, who often chose as his subjects lively figures and scenes from everyday life in the city's *calli* and canals.

Francesco Guardi, instead, developed his pictorial talent reproducing landscapes, thus anticipating the artistic output of **Giovanni Antonio Canal**, known as **Canaletto** (1697-1778). Both as painter and scenographer, Canaletto immortalized his city in bright and perspectively perfect images.

With the close of the 18th century, Venice's artists ***moved away from the city***. Even the sculptor **Antonio Canova**, who loved his city to the extent of brokering the restitution of San Marco's horses which had been purloined by Napoleon, left Venice for Paris and other European capitals. Venice, by then, was no longer the splendid Serenissima.

Portrait of the doge Niccolò Marcello by Tiziano Vecellio.

The World Of Culture

Venice was often a **refuge for men of culture** who, persecuted at home, found greater freedom in the city on the lagoon. The love of letters, together with the mastery of many of its artisans, also contributed to Venice's playing a primary role in **book publishing**. Soon after Gutenberg's invention of the **moveable-type printing press**, Venetian typographers, first among whom **Aldo Manuzio**, were able to produce at least half of all the books printed in Italy.

Of the various authors who were either born or spent extended sojourns in Venice, such as Pietro Bembo, Pietro l'Aretino, Paolo Sarpi, Gaspare and Carlo Gozzi, only to mention a few, here it is well to focus on **Carlo Goldoni** and **Giacomo Casanova**, two decidedly different personalities, but who were both particularly skillful at describing 18th-century Venetian society.

INDEX
LIBRORVM PROHIBITORVM
cum Regulis
confectis per Patres a Tridentina Synodo
delectos, auctoritate Sanctiss.
D.N.Pii IIII, Pont. Max.
comprobatus.

ROMAE,
Apud Paulum Manutium, Aldi F.
M D LXIIII.
IN AEDIBVS POPVLI ROMANI.

Title-page of the "Index Librorum Prohibitorum", *published by Paolo Manuzio, Aldo's son, in the second half of the 16th century.*

Carlo Goldoni was born in Venice in 1707, and manifested his love for the theater when still a young man, even though he was obliged by his father to pursue legal studies. He became familiar with and frequented theater-company managers, representative of that **Commedia dell'arte** which, in the preceding century, had spread from Italy to all of Europe, but was not recorded in definitive scripts. Every actor improvised following a so-called *canovaccio*, and usually concealed himself behind conventional masks. An acute observer of his time, Goldoni portrayed the apparently superficial world of the 18th century, graphically describing, with both irony and verisimilitude, the daily life of the Venetian bourgeoisie, with all its vices and virtues. Paramount among his masterpieces is *La Locandiera*, portraying a woman capable of efficiently and level-headedly managing her affairs. A count, a marquis and a knight, all three in love with her, represent a crisis-ridden nobility, incapable of coping with the competition by a simple servant, in turn symbolizing success-poised middle-class solidity.

A scene from the third act of La Locandiera, Carlo Goldoni's masterpiece, in a period etching.

Giacomo Casanova was born in Venice in 1725 and, unlike his fellow compatriot Goldoni, developed an interest in literature only at an advanced age, when his riotous career had by then finally come to an end.

The son of an actress, he was both a gambler and a card cheat, an impenitent seducer and unscrupulous adventurer. **Accused of practicing witchcraft** in 1775, he was locked up in the **Piombi** jailhouse, from which however he managed to escape. He then abandoned Venice and began wandering about Europe, both accumulating and dissipating an enormous fortune, and often keeping just one step ahead of the police. After having lived in PARIS, where he was a spy for the royal court, in SAINT PETERSBURG, where he met the Empress Catherine, without however managing to obtain the advantages he had hoped to enjoy by this acquaintance, and subsequently in LONDON and POLAND, he became the librarian of a noble Bohemian and set about chronicling his time in a book of **Memoirs**. The book mirrors both a wild and decadent society, but all in all not so different from that with which Goldoni too was familiar.

The Craftsmen

"From everywhere goods and merchants arrive, the latter buying whatever they want and having them shipped back to their countries. In that city you can find food in abundance, bread and wine, poultry and river foul, fresh and salted meats, large sea and river fish, merchants from every country, all buying and selling. In that fair city you can encounter the finest gentlemen, whose nobility is most praiseworthy, and their merchants who buy and sell; you will find there money changers and people from every walk of life; all sorts of seafarers, vessels capable of plying every sea and galleys to counter whatever enemy force. And in that most beautiful of cities many are the fair women and maidens, all richly attired..." This is how **Martino da Canale**, a 13th-century Venetian chronicler, described the daily comings and goings in his city, which at the time was well on its way toward reaching an unprecedented stage of development. It was the very ***laboriousness of the Venetians***, accustomed as they were to solving all sorts of problems and defending their danger-fraught territory, that proved the bedrock of a thousand-year history of a city

Below and opposite: *two views of the Arsenal of Venice, Europe's largest* fabbrica *up to the advent of the industrial revolution.*

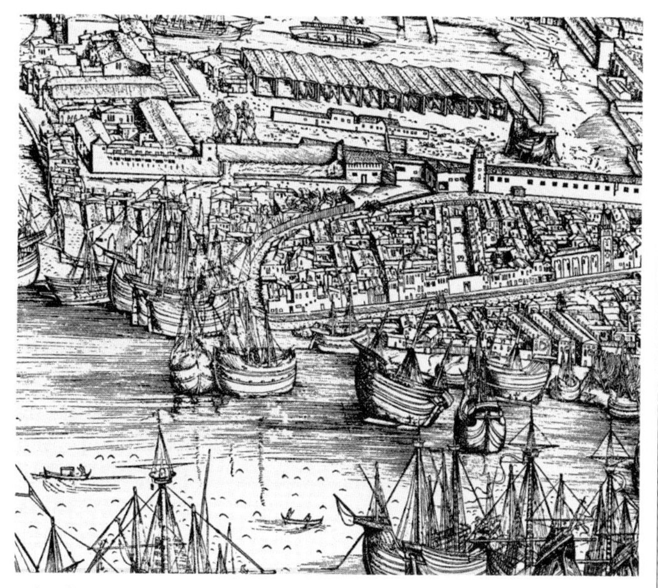

which was born in the middle of a swamp and which grew surrounded by the sea.

The **salt-workers**, **fishermen**, **vegetable growers**, **landowners** and **farmers**, the lagoon's first denizens who had fled from barbarian invaders, soon were flanked by **seamen**, **merchants**, **shopkeepers** and **craftsmen** who, starting in the 10th century before the development of other European medieval realities, had formed cooperative organizations know as **fraglie** and **collegi**.

Iron smiths, **coopers**, **glassblowers**, **butchers**, **skinners**, **basket weavers**, **dog** and **falcon breeders:** a lively and multicolored world constantly bustling about the *calli, campielli* or along the canals, or animating the docks of Rialto with its increasingly opulent market places overladen with all kinds of wares, but a world which was also able to blend and camouflage itself in the elaborate maze of its urban fabric.

It was the waters, both those inside the lagoon and the broader watery expanse of the sea, with their attendant demands, which, already in the 12th century, determined and shaped the development of Europe's largest *fabbrica*: the **Arsenal**, the very same that so sparked **Dante**'s imagination and which, as legend more than history holds, was built by **linking together** – via dove-tailed ramparts – **two twin islands**.

As time passed, and in step with the Republic's development, **the Arsenal increased in size**. Venice, in fact, based its livelihood on sea trade, and its ports were always teeming with ships. **Vessel, rope** and **weapons construction**, therefore, were the principal activities enlisting the skills of the **Arsenal workers**, the *arsenalotti* as they were known, who – in times of economic prosperity – numbered well over four thousand. The shipyard, organized along labor-division principles, was directly supplied by the Republic non only with raw materials and tools, but also with special overseers, whose task consisted in monitoring and ensuring output in the various work sectors. All the city's craftsmen, divided into guilds, had to alternately guarantee the presence of their representatives in the Arsenal.

Porters (*facchini*) would arrange the timber, which was then cut and sectioned by **sawyers**. After the wood had been shaped by **carpenters**, **caulkers** (*calafati*) then assembled all the parts produced in the various work units and proceeded to outfit the vessels. The result of this bustling activity were the **galley ships**, forty to fifty meters long and less than ten meters wide, which plied the ADRIATIC, the IONIAN, the AEGEAN and the BLACK SEA, together with rope and weapons, which ensured the survival of at least half of Venice's population.

Among the various guarantees these skilled workers succeeded in obtaining from the Republic, there was also an

Palazzo Giustinian at Murano, seat of an interesting glass-craft museum.

old-age subsidy, in every way similar to present-day pension schemes. Actually, the Serenissima wanted to avoid at all costs the transfer of its workers' skills and expertise outside the Venetian lagoon, which would only further sharpen the competitive edge of the city's foreign rivals.

Unfortunately, **after the battle of Lepanto**, at the very time when Turkish supremacy seemed to have been overturned, ***the Arsenal's business volume began to shrink***, thus causing **unemployment** for a large number of *arsenalotti* and hunger for their families.

The many hues of Murano glass.

If Venice developed the mythical Arsenal in the very core of the city, devoting to this area an increasing amount of space and sacrificing to it palaces and churches, the city was not similarly generous as regards another activity, that of **glass making**, another integral part of its livelihood from the very earliest times. In order to avoid the toxic fumes and fire risks spewing from and associated with the glass furnaces, in the second half of the 13th century the decision was taken to transfer these works to the isolated island of **Murano**.

With the frenzied activity of its furnaces, which turned out all sorts of goods, both for everyday use by the populace and the middle classes on one hand, and high-quality products to meet the demands of an increasingly sophisticated aristocracy on the other, Murano was able to **develop** to the extent of achieving a considerable degree of **administrative autonomy**, and in the 16th century, was even authorized to mint its own currency and give itself a series of autonomous laws.

Both the need and the will to **monopolize** production even led some master glassblowers to compile a series of norms, called **Mariegola** (1446), which clearly evince the extent to which the island identified with the glass makers' art. "The glassblowers' craft must have no other ambit wherein which to unfold than the sole island of Murano, where several centuries ago Venice transferred it, and where, being utterly self-contained, especially in terms of its workers and furnaces, this art can be both conserved and pursued..."

Rituals Of Pain And Glory

A characteristic which has helped make Venice world famous has undoubtedly been the vitality of its inhabitants, who from the very beginning displayed their willingness to play an active role in the events which were to shape the life of their city. These events ranged from the more solemn and determining to the daily but no less significant. **Saint Mark's Square**, the **Grand Canal**, the **calli**, **campielli** and **sestrieri**, veritable theaters wherein the borderline between protagonists and spectators was often blurred, were always full of **live** and **animation**.

All this can be gleaned from the **writings of the medieval chroniclers** who recorded the city's will to live and enjoy life's pleasures even in the most trying times. This is particularly evident in the **works of the major** 16th and 17th-century **artists**, those Venetian painters whose output often portrays aristocrats in close proximity to acclaiming throngs.

Similarly, this special atmosphere also came out in the **festivities** and **pageantries** which celebrated the Serenissima's most heroic events, or to hail the close of tragic ones, and which were actively attended by a cosmopolitan assembly, entranced by the pomp of the aristocrats' attire and grateful for the freedom they all enjoyed.

The "votive bridge" put up over the Grand Canal during the feast dedicated to the Madonna della Salute.

The procession, led by the Bucintoro, *left the lagoon in front of the Riva degli Schiavoni, and headed out to sea for the sea wedding ceremony.*

For centuries, starting from the year one thousand, that is from the time Pietro Orseolo II received an act of submission by the Dalmatians and Istrians, each year on the day of the **Ascension**, called the ***Sensa***, a naval cortege moved from the dock off Saint Mark's Square. The procession included the *Bucintoro*, the doge's boat, the gondolas of the nobles and rich merchants, the fishermen' boats, those of the *arsenalotti*, the workers of the Arsenal, and those of the populace. After reaching San Nicolò al Lido, the bells sounding over the lagoon, they ventured toward the open sea. The doge would then cast a gold ring into the waters of the Adriatic and pronounce the words: "We wed you, oh Sea, in token of true and perpetual dominion."

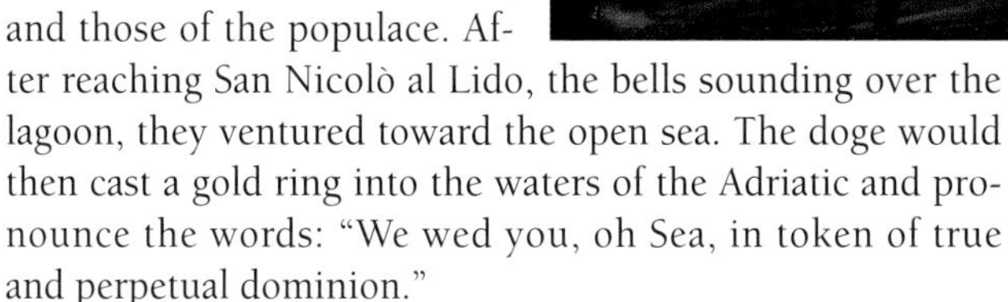

If the *Sensa* celebrated a glorious time for life in the Republic, the **feast dedicated to the Madonna della Salute** originated in response to a **vow** which was **made when a terrible plague** scourged the city in 1630. On the 22nd of October of that year, doge Contarini with the entire Senate decreed that, for fifteen consecutive Saturdays, there be held a procession in honor of the Madonna, and vowed to erect a church to the blessed Virgin, calling it **Santa Maria della Salute**, and that "every year on the day this city shall be freed from this present scourge, his Serenity and successors will solemnly proceed with the Senate to visit the same church in perpetual remembrance of public gratitude for the benefit received."

The church, designed by **Longhena**, was completed over fifty years later, in 1687. Still today, when celebrating feast commemorating the event, Venetians participate in great number in the traditional pilgrimage and light a candle before the image of the Virgin Mary on the main altar.

A Special Carnival

During the final decades of the 18th century, ***Venice is no longer the world's commercial hub***, but has nevertheless achieved ***great fame as a lively highlife center***. Theater foyers are the preferred venue for all sorts of gallant behavior, such as gaming, courting the ladies, and fixing rendezvous. Nary an evening goes by without some concert, show or some occasion to celebrate, and with no restraints of any kind. Every year some important guest arrives, and is welcomed with a display of pomp. In 1782 there arrive in Venice **Paul**, **Catherine of Russia's son**, his wife, and pope **Pius VI** on his way back from Vienna. In 1784, **Gustav III of Sweden** arrives and, while in France an epoch-making revolution was about to take place, in Venice, a special tourist destination for both popes and crowned heads, **Carnival dons the cloak of a seemingly endless feast**: five months (and sometimes even more), starting in October, during which anyone, whether doge or beggar, can mingle with the crowds, his or her identity **concealed by a mask**, almost as if to eliminate the social differences of a world where the power is firmly in the hands of just a few families.

Below: *detail of an 18th-century painting by Pietro Longhi.* Opposite: *masks of today and yesterday.*

If the merry-making goes on virtually with no interruption, on the days preceding Lent, when Carnival peaks and a colorfully festive crowd floods Saint Mark's Square, under the porticos of which there were by then **over twenty-five cafés**, a motley variety of Harlequins, Punches, Pantaloons and other typical "masks" find themselves elbow to elbow with fake nobles and would-be sailors, with an incredible variety of masks, fruit of the city's ancient artistic creativity, with jugglers, soothsayers and charlatans, all admiring the spell-binding acrobatics of the gondoliers who have arrived especially from Castello, or the *svolo del Turco*, a performance wherein a tightrope walker balances his way from San Marco's bell tower to the Loggia Foscara.

Every *piazza*, every *calle*, becomes a theater where circus shows and dances are performed and participated in by people of all social classes, to the delight of on-looking innkeepers, gondoliers, mask makers, tailors and others as make up the city's varied human panorama. Every palace along the Grand Canal fills with guests who arrive from the waters of the lagoon on vessels of every shape and size.

If this frenzied Carnival mood, at a particularly trying time for the city's economy, especially as it is now on the brink of losing its autonomy, offends the moralists, it nevertheless entails a series of significant advantages. This is why, when doge Paolo Renier dies on February 13, 1789, is demise is held secret until March 2nd, so as not to pall the festive spirit, thus filling the by now nearly empty pockets of those who profit from the amusement of others.

Table Of Contents

Finito di stampare nel mese di dicembre 1997
dalle Grafiche BUSTI S.r.l. - Colognola ai Colli (VR)
per conto della Casa Editrice DEMETRA S.r.l.